Protecting Your Library's Digital Sources

The Essential Guide to Planning and Preservation

MIRIAM B. KAHN

American Library Association
Chicago   2004

While extensive effort has gone into ensuring the reliability of information appearing in this book, the publisher makes no warranty, express or implied, on the accuracy or reliability of the information, and does not assume and hereby disclaims any liability to any person for any loss or damage caused by errors or omissions in this publication.

Composition by ALA Editions in Palatino and Optima using QuarkXPress on a PC platform

Printed on 50-pound white offset, a pH-neutral stock, and bound in 10-point cover stock by McNaughton & Gunn

The paper used in this publication meets the minimum requirements of American National Standard for Information Sciences—Permanence of Paper for Printed Library Materials, ANSI Z39.48-1992. ∞

Library of Congress Cataloging-in-Publication Data

Kahn, Miriam (Miriam B.)
  Protecting your library's digital sources : the essential guide to planning and preservation / Miriam B. Kahn.
      p.   cm.
  Includes bibliographical references and index.
  ISBN 0-8389-0873-X
  1. Libraries—Safety measures. 2. Archives—Safety measures. 3. Library information networks—Security measures. 4. Electronic records—Conservation and restoration. 5. Emergency management—Planning.
6. Computer security. 7. Data protection. 8. Electronic data processing—Backup processing alternatives.
  I. Title
  Z679.7.K385 2004
  025.8'2—dc22   2003023834

Printed in the United States of America

08 07 06 05 04   5 4 3 2 1

To My Family

Contents

Preface

Today libraries, archives, and organizations of every size are creating websites with digital materials that they maintain day in and day out. Some repositories are digitizing written works in the public domain and putting them on the Web and on CD-ROM (or equivalent technology) to make them accessible to the public, with the twofold aim of (1) providing access to the information today while preserving the fragile or rare originals for the future, and at the same time (2) wanting to "keep" the digital information for the future. Other institutions have created massive digital databases of their holdings, including books, manuscripts, and images that they want to be accessible on the Web. On top of all this is the incredible amount of office files, materials, circulation records, and cataloging records that are created every day.

The very largest libraries and archives in the world, in conjunction with national library and archive consortia, have been looking at the issue of the preservation of digital materials for several years. They have begun publishing "best practices" that any library of any size can incorporate into its project planning, budgets, and follow-up. Corporations and financial institutions have focused their energies on contingency plans and enterprise-wide backup of data.

Less well-funded libraries and archives and other cultural institutions need a practical "how-to" guide to plan for the future of their data, whether it be for access tomorrow, next year, or in ten years.

This book will look at the prevention of loss, the restoration of data or digital materials, and planning for long-term access to these materials. There are two major issues in planning to prevent the loss of digital materials: physical loss of data and hardware; and intellectual loss. Section 1 of this book will look at that common disaster, loss of data from a system or server crash, and how to prevent the loss of data through regularly scheduled backups. It will examine procedures to plan for the restoration of hardware and software after a loss and the salvaging of physical storage media and hardware. Section 2 of this book will discuss procedural decisions to increase the longevity of digital materials, documents, images, and databases. It will look at the digital preservation options of copying, migrating, reformatting, and converting. (Just because a library or archive stores information on a diskette, CD/DVD, or magnetic tape does not ensure that the data will be readable in the future, even as soon as tomorrow.) The discussion of project planning will include questions about what types of storage formats to consider, types of operating systems, software, hardware, "refreshing of data," and that all-important planning and budgeting for future supplies, storage, staff, and expertise to maintain the viability of digital materials into the future.

Chapter 10 of this book provides 29 different checklists to help digital project managers and information technology specialists formulate a disaster response plan and consider a variety of issues in planning for the long life of their projects.

Acknowledgments

Thanks to Cynthia Read-Miller and Jane Kenamore for ideas about individuals and their need to back up data. Thanks to Clark Searle for his help with insurance and the disaster response industry. Special thanks to Nancy Birk, former special collections librarian and university archivist at Kent State University, and to Julie Callahan, librarian at Columbus Metropolitan Library in Columbus, Ohio, for listening to my ideas about disaster response for libraries. Thanks to Tom Benjamin at Iron Mountain. Thanks to Robin Fremer who helped me through the rough days and Wayne Luff, my business partner, who helped me make time in my schedule to write. And most of all, thanks to my excellent editor, Marlene Chamberlain, for her editorial support and encouragement throughout the writing process.

Introduction

Despite the events of September 11, 2001, the power blackout in the northeastern United States and Canada in August 2003, hurricanes, tornadoes, and other disasters natural and otherwise, one out of every three businesses or organizations has no disaster response plan for digital resources and will not survive a failure of its computers or technology.[1] What we need are plans for and forethought on how to keep our operations functioning despite loss of data and computers. Creating plans to deal with a loss of computer data is essential to the future of libraries, archives, museums, and their parent institutions. Without that data, service cannot be provided, be it local or remote, and your patrons will seek information and assistance elsewhere.

In the same way, planning for the retention of digital materials is an essential part of protecting and ensuring the long life span of digital materials. It is also the key to an effective disaster response or contingency plan for computer operations. While libraries, archives, and museums have been writing or thinking about disaster response plans for years, they often do not think about the computer operations in their own buildings, let alone in the institution as a whole. What libraries, archives, and museums have usually considered is what to do if their audiovisual materials get wet in the course of a disaster. By audiovisual materials, I mean audio and cassettes both digital and analog; CDs in all their manifestations, DVDs, videodiscs, etc.; and LPs and their earlier forms. Some institutions may also consider photographs, negatives, microfilm, and microfiche to be audiovisual materials. To this end, the institutions consider how to determine whether the audiovisual materials are wet, and if they are, whether it is cost-effective to dry them out. In the case of all audiovisual formats, there are two questions to be answered: (1) is the object dry and clean so that a user can access its information; and (2) is playback equipment available either at the cultural institution or at the patron's home so that they can play the medium? These same issues apply to digital materials.

We have learned from the audiovisual field the importance of proper storage conditions, both physical and environmental; the importance of playing and copying the contents of the storage medium to ensure that "new" playback equipment can "read" whatever is on the tape or disc; and that some organization or institution should take responsibility for keeping the "last" piece of playback equipment so that future librarians and archivists can access the medium. The audiovisual preservation field has been very successful in its efforts to retain physical storage media and our access to them.

So now we must apply these lessons to digital materials. Digital materials come in many forms today and will continue to increase in number and complexity with each succeeding year. The professional literature describes digital materials in a number of ways, most often as either "born digital," that is, the data was never in any format but digital; and digitized or scanned, that is, the data existed in another format, print or three-dimensional, and is now accessible in some digitized format. In a true sense, born-digital materials are the most vulnerable to time and technological improvements because they were never anything else. Digitized materials are now in their new format for a variety of reasons, most often to provide access to the image or the intellectual content without further damaging or putting more stress on the original object. It is generally understood that the original object is not available to the casual user, just those who need to work with it for scholarly or research purposes.

So how does all this relate to protecting data? In a nutshell, if we don't protect the physical object from deterioration due to poor storage conditions and environment, then it will be impossible to access the data stored on that medium in the future. And if we don't take into consideration how we will access the data when the hardware, software, and operating systems no longer exist, then all that hard work is lost to future scholars. Data in the form of letters, reports, statistics, images, databases, catalogs, and full-text books, as well as every website that has ever been mounted and modified, are all at issue

and vulnerable to time and technological change.

As previously stated, this book is divided into two major sections. The first looks at protecting data and the physical object or medium from "normal," everyday losses from fire, water, careless backups, and computer or server crashes. In essence we will create a disaster prevention and response plan for computers and their data, as well as look at an overarching contingency plan for recovering the operations of the computer services and related departments in your institution. The second section will look at current practices for preserving digital materials and will define the methods used for "refreshing" data. We will also look at the issues of how future librarians, archivists, and computer technicians will access the data on current storage media, how the profession will try to ensure that it will be there later, and how we will pay for it.

The issues we will consider in this publication are different from those in most books entitled "preservation of digital materials" or "preserving digital materials." For the most part, these books discuss how to organize a project to digitize materials from print or three-dimensional formats to some digital format. They are not necessarily looking at digitization as a means of preserving the object from excessive handling and abuse or as a long-term storage and access issue.

Advertisers, the general public, and the promoters of these processes often use the word "archival" to imply preservation without differentiating these two terms. When talking about technology, it is important to understand what these terms mean colloquially and what they mean in the library/archive and information technology (IT) fields. When you *archive* data, it is stored in a retrievable, accessible manner for the long term. When you *preserve* data, the physical object or storage medium is stored for the long term under stable environmental conditions, but the data may not be readable or accessible. First we will explore the issue of keeping the data and its physical storage medium so that your organization can get to it if computers crash or your building is inaccessible. Then we will look at creating digital materials and storing them in an archival manner so that each item is retrievable in the future.

NOTE

1. Business First "Survey: Firms Unprepared for Operations, IT Outages," *Business First*, March 7, 2003, A27.

SECTION ONE

Why is planning for the loss of data so important? For a number of reasons, including the amount of time it takes to reconstruct the data the way it was originally created, accessed, or used. Think about how much time it takes to load your software and data onto a new computer. It takes many hours. What if you lost the data and software as well as the computer? Now think about how long it would take to order a new computer with all the features you want, get it delivered, purchase the software, install it, and then try to find your latest data backups. If you are like most people, you don't have all your data backed up, or you've only backed up older versions, original renditions, last year's data, or those special projects you could never live without. Worse yet, you might have backups for the data, but the only versions of the software you have are older and so you cannot read the files because software is never forward-compatible. And if you thought this could never happen to you, imagine what it would be like if everyone in your organization lost their data all at the same time, and each department had its own sense of how important its job is to the mission of the institution. But if you do some advance planning and are proactive about it, then you and the computer department will have a good idea of what is needed and where and when each function is slated for recovery.

There are several names for plans that you may have read about in "disaster response" or business literature: contingency planning, business continuity planning, emergency management plans, and disaster response, to name a few. Each aims to do the same thing: get operations back up and running.

"Disaster response plan" is the most common term used by libraries, archives, and museums. These plans deal primarily with recovering damaged books, audiovisual materials, photographs and paintings, and three-dimensional objects. While making decisions about the recovery of objects, the disaster response plan also discusses how to get both public services and behind-the-scenes operations back up and running.

Contingency plans deal primarily with computers and all related data services, such as fiscal operations and data transfer.

Business continuity plans look at how to keep the business as a whole running: operations, personnel, financial, and customer services.[1] The word "continuity" is used because if there are a multitude of plans at an institution, it is essential that the disaster response team members be aware of the other plans and their priorities for restoring services, and that the disaster response team leaders communicate with each other as they design, coordinate, and carry out their plans.

Emergency management plans usually fall within the jurisdiction of an emergency management agency and are discussed in conjunction with damage or destruction to a city or county infrastructure. Such efforts are often organized by law enforcement agencies in a state, city, or county and focus on restoring the operations of the government, public services, and infrastructure, especially after a natural disaster such as a tornado, flood, or hurricane.

Each of these types of plans has its trade literature and sources for specialized information.

Industry and planning information is found in the American trade journals *Disaster Recovery Journal* and *Contingency Planning and Management* and in the British publication *Survive*. Of course, you will find articles about disaster prevention and its many permutations in business journals, library/archive and records management journals, and almost every other type of publication. The World Wide Web is also a great place to look for general information, the names of organizations and service providers in your geographic area, and basic guidelines for plans.

As opposed to just "thinking about" disaster response planning for recovery of your three-dimensional objects and then designing a plan on the fly, you must be proactive about planning for the recovery and long-term retention of your data. *If* you do not plan ahead, then you are bound to lose what has been so painstakingly created, stored, and preserved.

NOTE

1. Jeffrey W. Greenberg, "September 11, 2001: A CEO's Story," *Harvard Business Review* (October 2002).

1

Preventing Common Causes of Loss

It will never happen here!

We've all heard this expression, but since September 11, 2001, the attitude it represents seems to be less of an issue. The further we get from that date, however, the more the denial syndrome will come back. Planning for the loss of data, and for retaining information over long periods of time, are the two best methods of ensuring that "it will never happen here"!

Where Libraries and Archives Are Today

Libraries and archives have been developing disaster response plans for quite a while now. This doesn't mean that every institution has one, but the number is growing, especially in the aftermath of 9/11. Institutions are looking at the need to protect their collections from any type of damage or loss. Unfortunately, libraries and archives are all over the board when it comes to actually having an up-to-date written disaster response plan.

When we look at disaster response plans for computer services and the electronic information maintained by libraries and archives, we again find that the preparedness levels of institutions vary. The degree to which a library or archive is computerized plays a large part in determining how prepared the organization is for the loss of access to computers and online data. Some electronic resources are backed up onto institution-managed servers and networks; some are not. Indeed, some of the most valuable data is stored on local hard drives and is backed up irregularly by the individuals responsible for those computers. This is the first issue of concern in this book: the protection of data and computers today, so that libraries and archives can function when computer systems fail.

There are three items to consider when examining how to protect your data for the short and long term. The first is *backing up the data onto a removable storage medium.* Item two is *storing the data in a safe, secure location.* The third item is *being able to recover the data* and *reinstall it onto the existing or re-created databases* your organization maintains.

It is important to realize that backing up data onto tapes protects the organization from loss of information as a whole. However, if you want to retrieve a *specific* piece of information, you must provide some indexing to go along with the data. In this way, you can retrieve the data without having to reload the entire tape. This is the difference between backing up data and an archival database. When you think about creating backup files, you might want to think about the long-term issues at the same time. For a little more time and money, you can accomplish both tasks at once, and save serious expenses over the long term.

Common Causes of Loss of Data

Accidental Erasure

Accidental erasure is probably the most common type of loss of data. This happens when you close a file and don't save it, or write over the original file when you meant to save it as something else. You might mistakenly delete a file, but if you don't do something else in between, and you don't turn off the computer, you can usually restore the file. Now if you erase or delete a file accidentally from a network, then you would need to have the computer systems department restore the file. They can only do this if the file has been backed up when the server is backed up. If you lose a file that you were responsible for backing up on your own hard drive, then you may be out of luck, unless it was on your backup tape. Anything you don't want to lose should be backed up onto some external medium (diskette, CD-ROM, tape, flash memory, etc.).

You can lose your current changes when there is a power surge or your computer crashes and you forgot to hit the save button. In this case, the computer might remember that the file was open and present the "last saved version" of the file. But if you haven't backed up the file since the day before, and you lose the current work, you may be out of luck and have to create all the changes again. It is this loss that is most costly for individuals and organizations to re-create. Worst of all, insurance policies don't cover this type of loss. (This issue is discussed in detail in chapter 6.)

Many computing departments leave the backup of individual data to the individual user. Unless your users are compulsive, they won't back up their own data regularly. One solution is to have all users' directories reside on the network so that data is backed up automatically when the system is. The only limitation here is the amount of memory storage capacity allocated to each person or account. Copies of individuals' data should be kept both in their offices and some other remote location, such as their car, home (if permitted), or the data center itself. Some mechanism needs to be in place to check that the storage medium is accessible, readable, and contains data. Storage media should be labeled with information that includes what type of data the medium contains, when the backup or the data was created, the programs used to create it, and whose data it is.

Viruses and Worms

Computer viruses and worms invade computers through unprotected computers via e-mail, diskettes, and CDs, where the unwitting or unsuspecting receiver opens an attachment. The most common computer virus invades your e-mail program, causing your computer to send out messages with the same attachment to everyone in your address book. Most of the time, you have no idea that your computer is sending out viruses until a friend lets you know. Other computer viruses attach to program files, causing the programs to perform improperly, while others infect DOS files, corrupting the operating system and requiring many hours of work to reformat the hard drive. You need to have your operating software on a bootable disc to regain control of the computer from the virus.

The best protection against unwanted viruses is to install antivirus software on your computer and your network. Once you install the software, it will check your hard drive, e-mail, and all files every time you open them. You can also check disks and CDs before installing or playing them. The antivirus software will update itself regularly and should be upgraded annually. Antivirus software companies include Norton and MacAfee.

Computer software companies and computer news services post fixes for viruses that you can download and install. The virus fix will remove the virus. In some cases, you will lose all your e-mail and addresses, especially if the virus is invasive and the cure is to reformat your hard drive. Back up your address book and bookmarks or favorites regularly using the export feature in your e-mail and browser. If your institution doesn't back up e-mail to tape banks, then back up your e-mail using the archive function on your e-mail program. Be careful to archive to separate disks or files, since the archive feature can write over existing data files.

Other computer viruses are called worms. Worms corrupt your hard drive by copying their files over and over again onto it until there is no space left. Once there is no space left on your hard drive, computer programs won't function.

Removing the worm includes reformatting the hard drive and restoring all the programs and files. If you haven't backed up your files and programs, you will have to re-create them, a most time-consuming chore.

Accidental erasures of data, viruses, and worms aren't the only types of loss that can occur, however. In today's technology-dependent world, the loss of power and of phone, cable, and Internet connections, let alone access to the computer itself, can become a major crisis.

Power and Telecommunications Outages

POWER OUTAGES

On August 14, 2003, just after 4 p.m., a blackout hit the northeastern United States and Canada, turning off computers, lights, and everything else from Long Island and Manhattan Island to Detroit, Toledo, and Cleveland and north into Canada as far as Toronto and Ottawa. The blackout brought airlines and trains to a halt; gasoline stations couldn't pump gas; some cities had no water, and restaurants and groceries did their best to distribute perishable food before it spoiled. Some businesses had backup power for 4–6 hours, others for 12 hours; some had diesel generators, but the majority of businesses just shut down. The blackout lasted anywhere from twelve hours to four days depending on where you were in the country. Some businesses had contingency plans so that their current data was automatically backed up to remote locations or generators kicked in, and their staff reported to an alternative operations site to begin repairs and the restoration of service.

To prevent the wholesale loss of data, an uninterruptible power supply provides battery backup to allow for time to close computer systems down systematically rather than have them crash and users lose their active data files. Some of today's programs will actually save files that are trapped on the computer due to system failure or power outages, but they only remember the "last saved version." When the system is restored, the computer system will ask if you

want to use the last "lost" version. Of course, you could set your computer to save regularly, especially if you are using stand-alone equipment. The main problem with auto-backup is that it will overwrite the current file again and again. If you are editing that file to become something else, as when you modify a template, the computer will overwrite the original version, and then you won't have the original in the backup. Develop a routine, if you are editing an existing file, to immediately save the file under a new name. In this way the auto-backup doesn't overwrite data that you wish to retain.

A large institution should have its computing systems running on at least two different power grids. That way if one grid goes down, there is another available for running backup servers and communications.

TELECOMMUNICATIONS OUTAGES

Loss of telecommunications is very frustrating in today's working and researching environment. Libraries and archives today access their external databases and information resources while hardwired to a T1 line (or something faster), ISDN, fiber-optic cable, or a cable connection. The internal network may be wireless or hardwired together and can include intranets, circulation systems, online catalogs, and other internal databases that are not accessible from outside computer systems. Very small libraries and archives may still be dependent upon dial-up service providers.

Regardless of what type of telecommunications system your institution employs, you should have some type of backup service for your communications needs. This goes for phone service as well. Some institutions have a few non-electric phones to use should the electricity go out; that way they can dial out for assistance.

Institutions need to think about some alternative access method to web-based and server-based systems when high-speed telecommunications connections are down, disrupted, or disabled. The alternative access could be by dial-up or another cable system. When reviewing your disaster response plan, you should think about using two different companies or access methods. But beware: all the telecommunications companies in your area may be using the same optical fiber network, so you may need to establish an agreement with a neighboring institution. You should investigate this thoroughly before signing any contracts.

Other alternatives for telecommunications may include contracting with an "on demand" wireless communications network that will provide you with e-mail and paging should the telecommunications in your area go down.[1] Of course, there is a caveat with this option. If there is a major disruption in the infrastructure in your city, as happened in New York City on September 11, 2001, then bandwidth for wireless communications may be jammed or unavailable for emergency contracts. If your institution thinks wireless communications are essential during a disaster or` loss of computer access, then you should think about a contract with a company that provides the "on demand" wireless service.

SUSTAINED LOSS

No matter how you plan to continue providing services during a power outage, should your institution suffer a telecommunications outage that results in loss of contact with the computer systems, then you must have an emergency plan in place to forward all phone numbers and lines to an alternative location. You must also have personnel at the alternative location to answer the phones. This is true of the telecommunications methods for accessing servers and networks in your institution. If you need to provide different access methods to the data over alternative data lines, then you need to write this into your plan, and establish a contract with a company that can provide the service. (Your computer disaster response team will need to get another mirror site operational or your original site operational as quickly as possible. Be certain to build in backups to the mirror site.)

If there is a sustained loss of telecommunications or power, your institution should declare a "disaster" with your data storage/backup service

provider and activate your disaster response plan for computer services. This would mean gathering the backup software and data and mounting it on computers and servers in a remote location. This facility can be near your facility or in another city.

After September 11, 2001, some businesses experienced a reluctance on the part of their employees to travel any distance from home. This resulted in the increased use of mobile recovery centers for data disaster recovery. When your organization declares a "disaster," all that practicing and testing by the information technology and systems department for the full restoration of data will come in handy. This will also be the time to offer your information and research services from a remote location and take queries by phone, fax, and e-mail instead of in person.

Regular Backup Procedures— What's So Important?

To forestall the loss of data and loss of patrons, let alone work product, regular backups are imperative. This isn't the only procedure to incorporate into daily routines. You must check that the backup system is functioning, both the hardware and the tape, and that the data and associated software are readable and usable. Otherwise, you will end up having to create the data again.

The whole idea behind data and program backup is to prevent loss of data from the computer system when the server or network crashes. Unlike disaster response planning for the physical items in a library or archive, you cannot create a response and recovery plan on the fly. Careful premeditated steps must be taken to ensure the safeguarding of data and computer systems. To this end, computer disaster response plans focus on the prevention of loss first and foremost.

When an organization loses its data, the financial implications can be enormous. One study examined the cost of lost data and concluded that "every cent of data backup is worth

$2500 of data re-entry."[2] Another cost study reported that employees on average cost $36 per hour; imagine the amount of productivity lost should your department, building, or institution lose its ability to access computer services for even one hour.[3]

Time studies show that for every hour of data lost, it takes one day to reenter it within the course of a normal workday; and for every day of lost data, it will take a week to reenter the data. Just think about the types of work you perform in the course of a normal day, then multiply that by the stress of performing work under less than normal conditions in a strange environment. Now add to this the loss of your data files and the need to re-input data and re-create original ideas, projects, catalogs, and websites. The reconstruction of data is time-consuming and extremely expensive, and many times can be avoided.

Types of Backup: What Method to Use

Business literature discusses two important issues to consider when selecting backup methods: the time it takes to recover the data and how much data loss you can live with; and the time it takes to get the operations back up and running.[4] Or to think about this another way, what is the cost to your institution of using or having old data, and what is the cost of being off-line? Can your institution survive with old transactional data? Do you even have any that is mission critical?

What type of backup method do you choose for your institution, building, network, or office? Well, it depends upon the resources (people, equipment, and money) your organization has, and how critical the data and the computer operations are to the survival of your institution. Two questions to ask the computer disaster response team are the following ones. How long can the institution, library, or archives do without computers? How long can you do without data before the amount of data to input is crippling? (Business calls these two factors RTO, or recovery time objective—how long you can live

without the application—and RPO, or recovery point objective—what is the maximum amount of data you can lose?)[5]

In the case of financial institutions, their data is so critical that even a few hours of downtime could destroy their cash flow, a crisis from which they might not recover. In the case of a library, archive, or museum, data is not quite as critical, although the institution as a whole might be more data-dependent. So what type of backup method do you choose? Well, if you need the data *now* no matter what the crisis, then your organization should be using data mirroring or replication. Data mirroring means that for every keystroke made, a mirroring keystroke is made in a remote location. So the data are almost identical. This type of backup is commonly employed by financial institutions, the travel industry, and other data-critical sectors. Other businesses use a fairly continuous transfer or backup of data, so the data might be shunted to another location every few minutes, or every hour. These incremental backups can be retrieved quickly but are more difficult to synchronize. Smaller businesses, archives, and libraries use data vaulting, in which the data is sent via the Internet, FTP (file transfer protocol), or TCP/IP (another type of transmission protocol) in regular cycles, but perhaps as slowly as every night. Tape and disc backup are still commonly used, store the least information, and take the most amount of time to back up, but are the least expensive to maintain. Tape and disc backup also mean that data is less critical to the survival of your institution, since reinstallation of the software and data can take between 12 and 72 hours, whereas data mirroring is almost instantaneous. No matter which method you choose for your institution, you must test the backup tapes to confirm that they are recording data and that the hardware is working.

Business continuity planners remind us that crisis management is better than disaster recovery, especially when dealing with loss and recovery of data and computers. If you have a plan and have backed up your data, the total cost to the institution of recovery is decreased by 25–50 percent.[6]

INCREMENTAL BACKUP

The most common backup method for individuals to use is the incremental backup. Only the files that have changed are copied onto some type of removable storage medium or a remote data storage site. These files are usually projects that people are working on or are critical data that the individual doesn't want to lose. At some point in time, the individual will back up everything, usually when they are switching to a new computer. Unfortunately, if the computer contracts a virus or a worm in the meantime, all the data that was not backed up recently, or ever, may be lost. Individuals should consider taking the time to back up their data on a regular basis, say once a month. That way what was a dormant project will not be lost.

Some automated backup programs also back up only what has been changed since the last time. This works well as long as a complete backup is performed on a regular basis, at least once a week. However, the organization runs the risk of losing all the data that was created since the last full backup. If the system that fails is your circulation or cataloging system, your staff may not be able to re-create the lost data.

Complete daily backup is the best method for smaller institutions that have automated systems, providing they can afford the loss of that day's data.

DATA MIRRORING

Data mirroring or replication includes synchronizing two or more data servers with exactly the same information. So with every keystroke or transaction you make, the same exact transaction is made to the second or third database. There are several types of replication that can be employed. The first is to back up or replicate on a second drive in the same cabinet. This would ensure against physical loss of or damage to the original drive. The second type of replication would be to have another drive or server in a different machine or power grid. This level of replication is common on a large campus. The third and highest level of replication is across geographical areas. This is also described as

"real-time" transaction replication. Some businesses in New York may replicate their data on the West Coast, or in Europe or Asia. The only caveat is the time it takes for the transaction to transmit from one location to another. The farther away the transaction has to go, the longer it takes, so these same organizations might have one local remote location and one far away. This is the type of real-time backup that is used by the financial industry and airlines.

Backup procedures always require scheduling, and checking that a backup was successful and the data is readable is an essential part of testing the backup.

Backup Media: What Format to Pick

Now that you have decided that you must back up your data and the method to be used, you will need to decide what removable or remote storage medium to use. There are several choices depending upon the amount of data you have, the frequency of backup, and how critical the data is to the survival of your institution.

Diskettes, CD-ROMs, and flash memory cards are great for the local backup of individual files and programs. But they have a limited storage capacity and you must perform the backup yourself.

Backup to tape in an internal drive is also a possibility. You have more storage capacity and can set the drive to back up automatically at the end of the day. These tapes may contain only the changed data or all of it, depending upon how busy your operations are and how critical the data is to your financial health. You should back the entire system up at least once a week.

You can also back up to a remote backup service provider. The data is transmitted over phone, web, or optical lines and is stored at that remote location. There are some advantages to this; it isn't next door and you could have the data restored at a different location, should your own location be unavailable due to a disaster. This could speed up your recovery process, provided you have planned for an alternative operating location.

You can also back up to a remote location that replicates your data as described above.

No matter what type of backup method you choose, don't forget the software applications. You should have copies or originals of these stored somewhere safe and off-site. What some organizations do to get around the issue of out-of-the-box software is to have one standard setup of out-of-the-box software applications for every computer station in their institution. Those are the only programs they load onto each and every system. If your computer dies, then they just bring a new computer with the same software applications setup and you reinstall your data and away you go. If you load your own software applications, then you had better have a copy to install yourself because it won't be supported by your IT department.

Selecting What to Back Up

You want to back up your critical data, your personal data, and any projects and databases you are working on. Think about how you would perform your job if your data was gone from your computer. If you cannot live without it, then it is critical. For example, the circulation system maintains a database of all books that are in circulation. There is a related database with all patrons' cards and personal data. If you restore the circulation system without the patron database, how will you check out books or get them back? Add to that the automated catalog and cataloging functions and see if the system is still operational. How does the loss of the catalog affect the circulation system?

NOTES

1. Message One and Blackberry are two of the companies that offer this service.
2. Frank J. Real, "Tick . . . Tick . . . Tick: Time Is Money When Recovering Lost Data," *Disaster Recovery* 15, no. 4 (fall 2002): 14–16.
3. Jason Buffington, "Data Replication Explained: Techno Advice for BC Pros," *Contingency Planning and Management* (May/June 2003): 58–60.
4. EMC Corporation, *A Symmetrix White Paper: Disaster Recovery as Business Continuity* (2002), www.emc.com/pdf/continuity/c894_disaster_recovery.pdf.
5. EMC, *Symmetrix White Paper.*
6. Peter G. Power, "Manage a Crisis, Don't Recover from Disaster," *Contingency Planning and Management Online* (January 2003): 22–26.

2

Planning
for the Worst

Loss of Computer
Operations

In the aftermath of September 11, 2001, the Federal Reserve, the Office of the Comptroller of the Currency, the Securities and Exchange Commission, and the New York State Banking Department met to draw up guidelines for the protection of data and the flow of information and monetary funds between U.S. financial institutions. Their concerns for computer systems were:

- rapid recovery and timely resumption of critical operations following a wide-scale, regional disruption;

- rapid recovery and timely resumption of critical operations following the loss or inaccessibility of staff in at least one major operating location; and

- a high level of confidence, through ongoing use or robust testing, that critical internal and external continuity arrangements are effective and compatible.[1]

In just the same way, libraries and archives need to be concerned with restoring access to their information and services for their patrons in a quick, efficient manner.

Keeping Up with the Changes

Software

Let's think about preventing the loss of data. What happens if you lose your data in a major server or network crash and it turns out that there isn't a current backup for the software. In fact, the software that you were using was the newest version of some program, and the computer center can't find that version and must use the previous one. Do you realize that you cannot open current data files with older software versions? You can do the reverse, of course: open old files with new programs. So here is another layer to add to backup routines and prevention programs: *back up the software.*

Of course, this disaster could be man-made if you "borrow" someone else's software, install it onto your computer (which is technically illegal unless it is freeware or shareware), and then your computer crashes and you find the only software you own is the older version. You are out of luck and lose all that time for data creation and access to your files, until you can purchase a new software program.

In the same breath, it is important to keep up with software changes. It isn't essential to purchase every upgrade, but pay attention to the industry. When it says that the new program no longer supports your software version, you have waited too long to upgrade and may have problems reading the old files with new software. Unfortunately the same rule applies to operating systems. If you wait too long to change to the new system, then you will find the data and its associated software won't run properly. In fact, this issue snowballs when you factor in the upgrading of your hardware.

When computers first became affordable, many cultural institutions delayed purchase until the "best" system could be found, only to realize that this was never going to happen. The institutions found that they had to buy into hardware and software, hope they had picked the right equipment and programs, and then get on the upgrade treadmill. If you don't upgrade your hardware when you upgrade the software, you may find that the technical requirements of the software are greater than your computing power.

To cope with the cycle of purchase and deaccession, some institutions lease equipment so they get automatic upgrades of hardware and software when the vendor comes out with new versions. As long as the costs for these upgrades are built into your budget, this works out quite well. Some institutions have instituted a purchasing cycle for hardware and software of anywhere from two to four years. IT departments probably upgrade more often than any other department, say every eighteen months. Support operations are upgraded maybe every three years. Don't establish a purchasing cycle greater than four years, or the technology and learning curve will be too great for your staff to comfortably absorb.

Operating Systems

What operating system are you using today? When did you make that commitment? What happens if you switch from MS Windows NT to Sun's Linux? How will you know which data is stored in which operating system? It is possible that different departments in your institution use different operating systems. Make certain you document any nonstandard formats, programs, and systems. Your computer services department staff needs to document the changes in operating systems, as does your records manager. This will be important for the future retrieval of or access to long-term digital materials.

Hardware

In the context of preventing loss of data, the protection of hardware should include preventing obsolescence. As software modifications increase computing power, your institution, building, and department may be forced to purchase new computer components. You do not need to replace all the equipment, but you need to make certain the older software and peripheral drivers can run the new configurations of hardware and peripherals. When you deaccession the hardware, make certain the hard drives are clean of

data by reformatting the disk, not just deleting the data. Check with your computing services department and ask them to help you with this.

What if your computer system is running old computer software on old computer equipment and you can't afford to upgrade? Then you will need to keep that old equipment running. It will also be necessary to find old components and scavenge for old parts. Think carefully about this issue because it is a very costly decision to stay with obsolete systems. The same holds true of homegrown or proprietary software systems. At some point, you will have to find the money and the expertise to convert to a new system. Doing this during a crisis is not the best use of your organization's time, money, and energy.

What will you do if the system fails; either the hardware or the software, or you have a disaster? Have you thought about where you will find the obsolete equipment and software? This is one of the most important reasons to back up your software, operating system, and data. If you are still running your programs and data in DOS or an older operating system and your system dies, you would be really lucky to find someone who has the right software and can help you restore your system.

Protecting Your Assets

On-Site Storage

It is common practice for individuals to keep backup files on diskettes or CD-ROMs at their desks while they are working on projects. It is a good idea to have additional copies stored somewhere else in case you cannot get access to the building.

Fireproof cabinets are designed for paper documents, and in some cases microfilm and microfiche. Fireproof cabinets are usually rated at 1,500–2,000° F. Magnetic media will begin to melt at 125° F. If this is your only method of storage, then you need to make certain that the fireproof cabinets will keep the temperature stable, and cross your fingers. The same goes for safes; they won't keep the magnetic media from melting. In both cases, the safe and the fireproof cabinet will not necessarily keep out soot, dust, and other airborne particulate matter. Soot and dust will settle on the surfaces of the magnetic media and then abrade these surfaces, causing loss of data should the medium be played prior to cleaning it.

Access to Backup Data

We have discussed the need to back up data and keep track of both the hardware and software required to read your data. Some questions to consider are:

> Where do you store the backups?
>
> How much of the system is on the backup tapes? And how often is it backed up?
>
> Do you store the tapes on top of the computer, in a "fireproof" cabinet in the room (both bad ideas), at home, in a physical data storage vault, in the car, with a vendor, at the bank?
>
> At what point do you send the backups from on-site or local storage to remote storage?
>
> Who can get access to the backups?
>
> Can you load the backups in a remote location or access the data from an alternative computing center?

These are some serious questions to ask yourself, the computer/information technology people in your department or building, and those at the institution. Set up a regular schedule for removing storage media from your desk or computer room to somewhere else. This way when there is a loss of data, the physical storage medium will be retrievable and the data can be remounted onto the network.

The departmental contact person should get together with the building computer disaster-response plan team leader to set up backup and storage schedules. The building contact should coordinate with the institution-wide computer disaster-response team for off-site storage protocols and procedures. These storage decisions should be coordinated with the institution's records manager. Discuss how the backup data fits within record-retention schedules for the institution as a whole.

Off-Site Storage

Just when do you transfer the data off-site? Data should be transferred off-site on a very regular basis. Often organizations will keep the most recent backup in their office or a nearby building, and then ship the backup tapes to the remote storage facility once a week. Thus the most current data, that which has been changed recently, is most vulnerable to loss. What might be better is to store the most recent week's data in another building, at someone's home, or even in the car if it isn't too hot or cold outside.

Then on a very regular basis, you want to send everything to the off-site storage facility. Send your data, software, and operating system software. Anything that you cannot live without should exist as a working copy in the remote storage facility.

You have several options for transferring the data off-site. You can physically take it or have it delivered to your storage facility. Many companies will arrange for daily or weekly pickup. You could send the data to a remote data storage facility via the Web, phone lines, or FTP depending upon how much data you have and where the facility is located. Of course, you also want to send the operating system and software to the remote data storage facility on a regular basis to prevent loss of everything.

Perhaps you have more data than is possible to back up every night. This is the case for large institutions, especially those that are extremely data-dependent. Well, there are some other options. In fact, you don't have to be a large organization to take advantage of a number of remote backup service products. So what are they? Well, there are remote backup services that accept your data via FTP or secured data-stream transfer on a regular basis. These businesses provide a software package that allows you to back up on a preset schedule to the remote location. Remote backup businesses can also describe their service as data vaulting. This industry has been around for at least fifteen years.

Data Storage Service Providers

Data storage services run the gamut from providing storage space for backup data tapes to hard-copy storage. Depending upon their sophistication and scope of services, these businesses may be associated with a disaster response company that can help you reload your data. (See appendix B for a list of companies that provide data storage services, etc.) For the most part, they are just storage companies with environmentally controlled areas for computer files. Some questions to ask when picking a data storage service provider include:

How quickly can you get access to the backups? If you need the data on a 24/7 basis, it is imperative that they provide services around the clock.

What are the costs and time frames for delivery?

Do you have to go there to pick up the tapes?

Are your data arranged in such a way that the storage company can find your tapes? Can they send the information via secured data line?

Can the data storage vendor provide a hot site or mobile recovery site if you need it?

Does the vendor have the hardware to set you up for a "declared" disaster?

Do you have the insurance coverage for this?

Can the data storage center find your "remote" or alternative location?

Hot, Cold, and Mobile Recovery Sites

"Hot sites" are facilities that are completely wired together with the hardware that your organization needs to get its information services up and running quickly. Organizations contract with these facilities to provide technical support should a disaster be declared. Hot site staff work with computer systems staff to test their disaster response plans in order to determine how long it will take to reinstall software applications and data. When computer systems crash or are unavailable, then the organization declares a disaster and computer staff head to the hot site. When the World Trade Center was destroyed on September 11, 2001, financial industries immediately declared disasters and their computer staff worked to get the companies' data operational as quickly as possible. Those that used data replication or mirroring had their computer services shunted to remote servers and were active almost immediately. Hot site time is traditionally paid for by the computer rider in your insurance plan, although the contract for the hot site is separate insurance and is paid for by the institution. The duration of stay in the hot site is limited by the size and scope of the disaster and the amount of insurance carried.

"Cold sites" are wired computer rooms without the hardware. These facilities are usually rented when the computer staff needs a long-term facility from which to operate.

Mobile recovery sites seem to be the most popular today, especially with small to medium-size companies. These facilities are movable trailers that are wired for telecommunications or have satellite communications for the user. The computer staff arranges to have the mobile recovery site delivered to a nearby location and computer operations are moved to this facility. Companies might use mobile recovery sites if their facility experiences water damage, sustains a loss of infrastructure in the immediate area, or needs a temporary facility during construction or renovation. Some companies are looking at mobile recovery sites as an alternative to hot and cold sites, thereby saving their employees the stress of temporary relocation during a disaster.

Protecting your data from loss is the key to your contingency plan. Continuity of operations and services is important to the survival of your organization. If you don't think about how you will get up and running again if you can't get into your building, then you may never restore the data or the services. Most important is updating your computer disaster response plan when there are changes in operations, procedures, or programs in your computer departments at any level of the organization.

NOTE

1. Board of Governors of the Federal Reserve System, Office of the Comptroller of the Currency, and Securities and Exchange Commission, "Draft Interagency White Paper on Sound Practices to Strengthen the Resilience of the U.S. Financial System" (Washington, D.C., August 30, 2002), www.banking.state.ny.us/ce0230830.htm.

3

Basic Considerations in Disaster Response Planning

Disaster Response Team Members and Their Responsibilities

All disaster response and contingency plans have a built-in complexity and various layers, no matter what their approach or subject. When it comes to protecting data and electronic resources, there are many layers of responsibility that add to territoriality within an institution. All the layers of administration and responsibility must work together cooperatively to achieve success in restoring data quickly and efficiently. Think about the various levels and departments at your institution and how they interconnect. You might start by looking at the organizational charts for your library or archive and for the institution as a whole. These are the various layers of planning that must be coordinated.

Each level of hierarchy has its own priorities for resuming services. Each hierarchy will have its own head of disaster response team, all of whom should communicate with each other, coordinate actions, and bring up systems within the prescribed prioritization plan conceived

prior to disaster. Coordination of the activities within each level of the hierarchy is important, as is the need for coordination and active communication between the levels of hierarchy within your organization.

Who should be involved in the planning process? Certainly representatives from departments who deal with computers and electronic resources should be included. Others to invite to a coordinating meeting are those people who create data or records, records managers and webmasters; and those involved with the computing infrastructure, people from departments such as strategic technologies, academic computing, digital repositories, and digital archives. The number of people involved at your institution may be two and may be twenty. All can provide input and perspective in creating a plan for protecting your data and its associated hardware and software. Each participant may feel that they have to create a plan for their department's needs. No matter what, the plans must have coordination points where priorities and resources are shared across the institution.

When you begin to designate disaster response team members, you will want one person per type for each job or persons who can perform more than one job. Depending upon the size of your computer operations within the institution, you will have one person coordinate the disaster response team at the building and network level, and three or four people overall. Everyone will be involved in the data recovery operations, but only a few people will coordinate the steps and priorities for restoration of services. Each team member will have an assigned responsibility to coordinate recovery actions.

A computer disaster response team should thus consist of three or four people with the following responsibilities. The smaller your staff, the more you may have to rely upon outside assistance or one team member performing multiple tasks. (See also checklist 10.)

> The team leader who is responsible for day-to-day operations, coordinates priorities and operations, and serves as liaison with the other disaster response teams

The remote operations person who is responsible for retrieving the backed-up data and loading the software applications and data onto remote servers

The local operations person who is responsible for recovering the hardware and storage media stored on-site and ordering new hardware, if necessary, to facilitate the reconstruction of networks and reconfiguration of hardware

The troubleshooter to facilitate remote access and assist reference and information staff with questions about temporary or new computer configurations

Be sure to have some people on the team who live nearby and some farther away. That way if the local infrastructure is affected, those who live farther away can activate the plan from the remote location. Those who live nearby may have to deal with family issues such as damage to their own homes, limiting their ability to assist during the first few hours of a disaster.

How are the various aspects of the plan going to be integrated across institutional, departmental, and administrative lines? There will need to be some serious discussions about who is responsible for what operations and services and at which levels. Coordination is the key to successful data recovery.

Planning at Each Level

Let's take a simple organization with three levels of administration. We'll start at the beginning and design a plan for all the different levels of computer use in the library or archive and work our way out to the institution as a whole.

Today libraries and archives have electronic data, information resources, and computer services in all departments and buildings. Staff gain access to various types of data from different computer systems without really thinking about where the information is housed. The basic plan will be the same, but the players will be different

at every level of this integrated plan. There are several issues to remember that relate to this plan. First is that the library or archive probably already has a disaster response plan for recovery of the physical objects in its collection, but this plan doesn't include computers. Second, the institution probably has a plan for computer services as a whole, but this plan might not include the library or archive functions and if it does, they will be near the bottom of the plan's priorities. Lastly, all departments and disaster response teams have to work together cooperatively, or recovery will take a long time and information may be lost. Cooperation is the key, for each department and institutional function has its own priorities for restoring service and computer data.

Job sharing and allocation between the institution's IT/computer data center and the information and technology people in the library/archive itself are common. The crossing of functions in IT departments seems to be more widespread on smaller academic campuses but can exist anywhere. The issue is control, of course, but the question of which department does what in terms of backup, remounting data, data and software integrity, and disaster response/contingency planning is important. Conflicting job priorities are also common and need to be worked out as you develop your disaster response plans. Priorities for the restoration of computer services and data will always be argued between departments and managers. Think about the mission of your institution and the impact that a loss of computers, data, and cash flow will have on the functioning of each department. The greater the impact, the sooner those operations should be restored.

So let's start at the simplest level and work our way to the most complex.

Individuals and Departments

First, either you or your department has a computer that holds various types of data that pertain to your responsibilities, administrative duties, and your department's collections. This

computer has correspondence, memos, e-mail, handouts and leaflets, databases, and maybe a small website or the backup for the department's website that is mounted somewhere else. This computer may also contain employment records, payroll information, your browser information and all the sites you have bookmarked, as well as your contact file or address book. What would we do without all of this vital information? For a stand-alone computer, there is usually one person in charge of the computer; it might be you, the administrative assistant, or a technician. In many cases, stand-alone computers are serviced and maintained by one person in the department or the library/archive.

The first step in your disaster response plan is to back up the data on a regular basis. You will have to decide how often that is: daily, weekly, monthly, quarterly, or whenever you remember. (See checklists 17 and 18.) The best schedule, of course, is daily, but only the most compulsive people will back up an individual hard drive so regularly. You should back up at least those files that have changed since the last time you backed up the computer. This is called an incremental backup. The backup can be on diskette, tape, CD, or even a removable memory chip. Some organizations may back up to a virtual data vault; more on that later. The worst place for the backup is in the computer; the next worst is next to the computer. You should have a separate location for the backup tapes or diskettes.

But your computer is part of a network. Isn't the data automatically backed up by the network? *No!* Only if the data is stored on the network will the data be backed up by the system. Any data stored on your hard drive isn't included in the global backup. *You have to do it yourself.* Too much trouble? Then don't keep anything on your hard drive, or purchase a software package that automatically backs up the data on the hard drive. You can set the software packages to back up daily or weekly. These software packages can back up some or all of the data, usually the data files that have changed since the last backup. Of course, you also want to make certain you have copies of the software stored safely in a separate location.

Using space on the server leads to different issues, such as the fact that the computing center gives individuals and departments a limited amount of space for storage of data, e-mail, files, databases, and so on. When you use up the space, you have to "archive" the lesser-used files, thus the practice of storing data on your local system or on a portable or removable storage medium.

You should back up your entire system on a regular basis, let's say once a month, with daily and weekly backups of changed files. Your databases and websites should be backed up every time you add data, and those backups should be stored in a separate location.

Consider adding simple metadata to your files. The metadata can be as simple as filling in the blanks on the "properties" box for each file you save. The "properties" box is located under the FILE menu in most software programs. You might want to include the subject matter of the file, creation and modification dates, and the purpose of the data. Metadata can also be a "read-me" file with a similar name saved in ASCII or Basic Text created on your WordPad that describes how to use a database, its basic characteristics, the programs to use with the data, when it was created, how it has been modified over the years with new features and software, etc. The metadata should help you identify the data in the file. Another piece of information to include is a description of how you created the original file and saved it in a new format or with a different program. Digital archivists use this metadata to track the history and provenance of files, especially those born digital.

Let's digress a minute to discuss why local data backup is so essential. It is ever so easy to get a virus or a worm or to overwrite a file. If the virus or worm corrupts your hard drive, which is what it is designed to do, then you may not be able to retrieve the data and *all* of it may be lost when the virus is removed or the hard drive is reformatted. In the same breath, you must keep your virus-checking software current, updated, and active so that it scans everything going into and out of your computer. This is imperative on a local, network, and system level. (See case study 1 at the end of this chapter.)

There are two other items that should be backed up: your software application and your operating system. You should have the original version of the software that is installed on your computer stored in a separate, safe location. A copy of the serial number or license number should be stored with the original and in another location. If you should lose your computer due to electrical failure, water or fire damage, or theft, you will need the original software or its license and serial number to install the program on a different computer. If your computer becomes infected with a virus, you may need to reformat your hard drive and then reinstall all the software. In this case, you will also need the original software. If your organization has modified the software in any way, or is working with older versions, you must have extra copies of the modified software and operating system stored somewhere safe.

In addition, you will need to back up the operating system software. The operating system is the software that tells the computer how to perform basic operations such as save, display information, write and read files to the hard drive, and many other behind-the-scenes functions. The standard operating systems today are Windows 95, 98, 2000, ME, XP, and NT for IBM-compatible computers. Other operating systems are Linux and Mac OS 10. If you are using an older operating system, it is imperative that you have a copy of that program backed up and stored with your software and your data. Some institutions have even designed their own operating systems or have modified them beyond the manufacturer's original design, thereby making the operating system or software proprietary. You must have backups for these proprietary systems and make new copies on a regular basis and *every* time you modify those proprietary programs.

In today's fast-paced computer software development market, software and operating systems become obsolete before your realize it. The standard upgrade cycle is eighteen months. Windows 95 is not 100-percent compatible with Windows XP (introduced in 2002). What is more of a problem is that even though you can open a Windows 95 file in XP and read it, the newer software will also reformat the data to fit its requirements. Then (1) the file is *not* the same as before, so you lose some of the history; and (2) you cannot read that file again in the earlier version of the software if you just save the file without renaming it. Types of data that are changed might include tables, forms, fonts, colors, and embedded images. This is an issue of obsolescence and also of compatibility. If the older version doesn't translate smoothly, you can risk losing everything. Make certain you save the "new" version with a different name or number than the original so that you can track the file's or data's history.

Prioritizing the Recovery of Individual Computers

Now that we have established that you must back up your own local data, we move onto the next responsibility of the individual or department. You need to decide how fast your computer system needs to be up and running. Immediately is not always an option, but a remote location or remote access may be. So you need to think about when in the scheme of operations and services the stand-alone computer needs to be back in service. Discuss the order of restoration of departmental computers with the individual selected to maintain and troubleshoot computers in your department. Depending upon the institution, that person can be responsible for backing up the data, fixing the problems, finding lost files, and everything else. Or they might just be the computer "expert" in the department. This individual should call someone else for help if they can't fix it themselves. The person they call might be responsible for the network's, building's, or institution's computers, depending upon how large the institution is.

The priority of recovering operations and data for a stand-alone computer depends upon the nature of the data and the services that position provides. In small institutions, the stand-alone computer may hold payroll and other fiscal services. In a museum, it might contain the records of the registrar, a catalog of those items

owned by the museum, their provenance, value, picture, disposition, and location. Or the computer may be the *only* computer in the entire one-person library/archive with everything on it: catalog, database access, financial records, and correspondence. How much data is on your computer and how important is it to the mission of your department?

Other issues to consider are: how can this department provide service without a computer and its associated data? Who else can provide the same type of assistance? Can the department use another area's computer? What are the manual operations for lost services like? For example, can the reference desk staff provide assistance and access to the collection without an online public access catalog? How does the circulation desk staff handle checking out books without a computer? (See checklist 13.) Most circulation department staff have a manual system for book checkout. They write down the patron's ID number and then all the bar code numbers associated with the books for checkout. When the computer system or the electricity comes back up, they then input each item into the circulation system. The books that were returned are also checked in. If the computer has been unavailable for a long time, more than a few hours, this becomes an enormous task with books piling up and off the shelf. The rule of thumb for input time is "for every hour of lost data it takes one day to input the data, in the course of a normal business day; and for every day of lost data, it takes one week." How long can your library afford to be without computer services or data?

If several stand-alone computers are out of operation, which ones are repaired first? Does the institution or building have extra computers it can switch out for the damaged ones? Who will install all the data? The task of the computer disaster response team is to prioritize the order that computer services are restored on the local level based upon function, interdependence, and contents. Their other job is to be prepared for action when the computer systems fail. (See checklist 25 for suggested criteria in evaluating restoration importance.)

The Network- or Building-Level Plan

Now let's look at a networked system in one building. How does this differ from a stand-alone system? The networked system shares items in common such as printers, fax machines, scanners, modems, and of course, data. It is the central location for the network operating system, software applications, files, and databases for a network or a building. In this case there are two places data can be stored; on individual computers with the software residing on the network server, or on the network itself. If the first is the case, then the individual is responsible for backing up their own data and sending the backup to storage or to the network server as discussed above. If all the data is stored on the server, then the operator for the network is responsible for scheduling the backup of all the data, software applications, etc.

There are some serious questions to consider when looking at a network backup. First, what type of data is going to be backed up and when? The backup will probably be incremental on a daily or hourly basis, i.e., the files that are changed today are backed up today. A full backup will probably take place on a weekly basis, with a backup of software applications and operating systems on a less regular basis. You will need to determine how long to keep the incremental backup of data files before reusing the tapes. There have been cases of tapes being reused too soon and weeks of data being lost when some important data element is sought and found to be accidentally deleted.

It is absolutely imperative that the backup tapes be checked periodically to confirm that the files are readable, and full backup tapes should be kept for at least one to two months before they are reused, if ever. If the backup tapes don't work, then you haven't saved the data!

Tests should be run to determine several things and the results noted in your plan. (See also checklist 14.)

How many people know how to reinstall software and hardware in the building? Are the procedures written down anywhere? If so, take them out and see if the steps make sense to the staff. If you cannot figure out how to install the software and data on a quiet day, how will you do it in crisis mode?

Determine how long it takes to back up the data every day and every week.

Determine how long it takes to find a lost or accidentally deleted file and restore it. This is particularly important if the backups are incremental. Document the steps so you can duplicate the process when the situation is hectic.

Determine how long it takes to install everything on a new hard drive, from reformatting the hard drive, installing the operating system and software, to reloading the associated data. This takes a lot longer than you think. A stand-alone system can take anywhere from four to eight hours to install just the software after a crash or a virus. The data, if it isn't lost, will take even longer to reinstall.

If you use a remote data storage company or have a contract with a hot site or mobile recovery site, then you should test the plan at least once a year to check the procedures and time for the installation of hardware, operating system and software applications, and data onto new computers.

An important item to discover is where the library/archive fits into the data recovery efforts of the institution as a whole, and when does your dedicated staff have to do some of the work on their own?

Prioritization for a Building or Network

For a building-wide failure, the computer disaster response team should know the necessary hardware for reconfiguring the local network or networks; installing all the appropriate operating systems and software; and reinstalling the data, databases, electronic resources, and their attendant links to remote servers and the institution-wide computers. Building-wide networks in libraries and archives include unique and shared electronic resources and reserves, local resource databases, and online local catalogs and circulation systems. There may be a separate network for all the offices and individuals in the building or department that forms a network for individual data that is not shared with the general public.

The building-wide disaster response team should get the network systems restored, then assist individuals with reinstallation of software and data on stand-alone systems. The priority here is to get the local network up and running so that the building or department is functioning at peak efficiency and providing excellent service. Depending upon the scope of your disaster and how the computer systems are affected, individuals could be given the option to work at home or at another location using remote access to the network while waiting for their stand-alone computers to become operational.

Now the building disaster response team needs to collect more information and prioritize the order of restoration of services and data depending upon the mission of your department and the importance of service to your patrons. (See checklist 25.) In a public or school library, you want to restore the circulation system first before all other systems. This is the heart of the institution. A university and research library may decide that some other function is more important. Circulation's functions are the most time-consuming to re-create. Next you might consider restoring the online public access catalog, the reference/electronic databases, and the website with all their interconnectivity. Cataloging functions can come later. Somewhere in the mix, you will have to restore the administrative functions of the computer system, including intranets, financial services, and human resources.

Something else to think about with regard to circulation systems is that there are stand-alone circulation systems that are used by bookmobiles. The data is then loaded into the circulation computer in a batch mode when the bookmobile returns to its base. This may be an acceptable alternative for smaller library systems.

Institution-Level Plans

On the institutional level there are many more factors to weigh than on the local level. This is the most important level to understand and to work with during the planning process for the computer services disaster-response plan. The institution probably has a large computing center that is responsible for all the computers in the organization. The center's function is to keep the networks and services as well as the mainframes and supercomputers running. The staff back up the system very regularly; many organizations have instantaneous backup, sometimes defined as a mirror site. Airlines, brokerage firms, and banks have systems with mirror sites, so that for every keystroke or transaction the identical activity is performed instantaneously in some separate and distant location, as was discussed in chapter 1. Should a computer system go down, the remote computer automatically takes over, or operations are switched to remote locations when disaster declarations are called in. This was the case for many brokerage firms and businesses on the morning of September 11, 2001. According to an article in *Newsday*, Comdisco Inc. received 39 disaster declarations in the first 55 hours after the World Trade Center was attacked. The first call came within 20 minutes of the attack.[1]

The computing center is responsible for the maintenance of the entire system, its ability to communicate with other computers on the same system, and the data contained therein. It is this last point that is crucial for the survival of the library or archive's computer system. Which group of computer people is responsible for backing up your digital archives, electronic reserves and journals, the databases, OPAC, and other types of shared resources? How well do the building- and organization-wide computer people communicate and interact? What institutional priorities and computing resources must be restored before others? Where does the library/archive fit within the institutional priorities? These are some of the serious questions to ask during this planning phase of your computer disaster response plan.

Prioritization and Responsibilities at the Institution Level

When the institution-wide disaster response plan is developed, where do the library/archive services with their associated physical objects and computing services fit within it? Someone from the library/archive disaster response team should be on the institution-wide planning team, or at the least there should be a liaison to the team. Not only is it essential for the library's computer disaster-response plan to fit within the institution-wide disaster response plan for the restoration of services, but the institution-wide plan must account for all the hardware that is in use in the library or archive.

The computing center's disaster response plan will include a contract with a data recovery services company to prepare against the loss of infrastructure at the institution, i.e., loss of power or telecommunications. These companies offer hot, cold, and mobile recovery sites for operating in "disaster" mode. In the event of loss of your computer operations, or lack of access to your institution as a whole, the organization declares an emergency and has computer staff along with backup tapes and files or remote data backups delivered to the data recovery company. The software and data are then mounted in this alternative site and operations should be restored using remote access methods until you can get access to your permanent facility. Testing the time it takes to do this full restoration is important. (See checklist 16.)

As discussed in chapter 2, a hot site is a room that is already wired for power, telecommunications, and with your specified hardware. All you need to do is load the software and files. A cold site is an empty room that is wired for power and telecommunications, but you order rented equipment and then mount your files. A mobile recovery site is just that, a work trailer with power and telecommunications as well as computers that can be moved to your location. Mobile sites seem to be the trend for smaller organizations. Large organizations will opt for a hot site for awhile. This is what happened in the first few days after the destruction of the World

Trade Center towers on September 11, 2001. With the declaration of a disaster, spaces were fitted with computers and the other necessary hardware to operate businesses.

Data recovery services companies, such as SunGard Worldwide, Strohl Systems Group, and Comdisco offer a variety of plans to suit your institution's computing and operations needs. (See appendix B.) This special type of insurance is vital if your institution is data-dependent. Data recovery service companies also offer and assist with the annual testing of your software and disaster response plans. Your computer staff runs a mock disaster and practices doing everything from gathering the staff and contacting the data storage facility, to installing and activating all the software and data at the hot site or mobile recovery site. Most often the testing consists of practicing pieces of the data restoration plan or the procedures, not recovering the whole system. Even if you decide not to contract with a firm, you must test the procedures and techniques for restoring software and data on a regular basis. If you do contract with a firm, read the service agreement carefully. You want to know where your institution fits within the firm's priorities for restoration,

should there be a regional or wide-area disaster and large commercial institutions declare disasters when your own cultural institution does.

Part of the computer disaster response plan is to decide who is responsible for local (building) maintenance of databases and hardware and who takes care of the computer system as a whole, its software, computer network, backups, etc. Who responds when individual computers crash? When the system crashes? When the hardware or software dies? When there is a virus or worm? Who deals with internal network problems, with electronic resources? (See checklist 4.)

How do you juggle the library/archive's needs with the needs of the institution? Are their different priorities or levels of response for "routine" problems versus disasters?

Working all these territorial issues out ahead of time is crucial for the smooth recovery of your computer operations and data.

NOTE

1. Monty Phan, "Companies Try to Retrieve Data," *Newsday*, September 19, 2001, A39.

CASE STUDY ONE

Backup Is Rule Number One for Secure Data

It's late in the afternoon and you are working at your e-mail correspondence when you get a message from a colleague with a cute attachment. Without thinking about it, you open the attachment and then scratch your head, wondering why that friend sent you such a strange letter. Without much more thought, you file away the e-mail and continue on with your task. Next thing you know, someone sends you a message informing you that there is a virus attached to your messages. Yikes! Why didn't the virus checker catch it? You look up the information on the Web that describes the virus and try to install the file so that you can run it on your computer and remove the virus. A few hours later after many choice cuss words, you get your computer clean and think that the virus is gone. A hard look at the virus checker shows that it was old and not renewed or updated, so you go out and get a new program and promise to update it diligently. You breathe a sigh of relief and count yourself lucky. And so, with an attack of the "I could have lost everything," you back up every file and become compulsive for maybe a month, until you go back to your usual routine of sporadic backups and housekeeping. Yes, you were lucky.

One day not too long after your crisis, a friend calls to say that their computer is infected. So you relate your experience, but this time the friend's computer has a major failure and becomes infected by a new virus that the virus checker companies haven't encountered and it has crashed the system completely. The operating software will not load. The hard drive will have to be reformatted and all the software reinstalled. After hours on the phone, the computer support person will ask your friend to use the "Restore Disk." Now your friend has to find it amidst the multitude of CDs and diskettes.

Depending upon how large your system is and how old your computer is, reformatting the hard drive could take two or more hours and you have to reinstall the operating software (Windows, OS, Linux, or whatever your system is running on). After that, you install all the software applications. This can be problematic if you downloaded and installed software from the Internet. You need to make certain your web connection is functioning right away. Another problem you may encounter is installing the software application more than twice on the same machine. Microsoft has new licensing restrictions that prohibit the installation of software more than twice. A quick call and explanation to their customer service center fixes that problem. Then you copy all your data back onto the hard drive, or at least what data you had backed up. By working nonstop, you get the system up and running in less than twenty-four hours. And you promise to be more vigilant in the future about backing up data, because you lost some files that were important and were never backed up anywhere but on the hard drive.

So what do we learn from these two scenarios? You have to back up your data, especially the active data, but even the dormant data, on a regular basis. Good housekeeping and backup practices include backing up data and files regularly, and removing files you don't use often and storing them on a removable storage medium. Store the disks somewhere accessible, but not right next to the computer. Make another copy and store it off-site. The system and software application discs also have to be stored somewhere accessible. If you don't have the software, how will your computer operate? This is crucial for effective restoration of your system. If you are working in a small institution and purchase your hardware locally, from a discount house or via mail order, you must make certain that the operating system and software discs are included with each and every computer or with each license. No matter how new your computer system, the software becomes obsolete within eighteen months to three years. If you have an older system, the software may not be available and your hardware may not be powerful enough to handle the new technical requirements of the new software. Regular backups and good housekeeping practices are just as important as a current, active virus checker. You can never back up too often.

4

Disaster Response Planning

As we discussed in the preceding chapter, information technology and computing centers all have a part to play in disaster response and recovery of data. There should be intersecting points for all computer disaster response plans. Separate plans are needed for each building and type of operation, with coordination between the two levels of planning: building and institution. The plans should indicate where the overall institutional disaster response plan fits into the local plan and vice versa.

The Plan

There should be a plan for each computer network, each department, and for the overall institution computing services. The interrelationship of these computer services was discussed in chapter 3. Each plan should indicate what the priorities are for restoring various networks and systems when the computers are affected on the local level, building level, institution level, and maybe even the city level. The computer disaster response plan should coordinate the restoration of computer services with the disaster response plan for preserving "physical collections." In this way, you can adjust the priorities of working on various systems and allocate staff where they are needed.

All the various types of disaster response plans should be clear and concise. You are writing procedures. Procedures should be written in simple language that anyone can understand and follow. Test the steps on team members who are not familiar with your computer systems. Build in "quick time" decisions to deal with unusual circumstances. You might even put together a decision tree that helps disaster response team members organize the order of computer services recovery. Priorities for the recovery of data are discussed in chapter 3 on preventing loss of data.

Vendors

Part of your plan includes replacing hardware and software applications that are damaged or destroyed during a "disaster." Look at where the supplies and resources will come from. Who will you order from if the entire city or county is affected by the same disaster? If the infrastructure of your geographical area is disrupted, then every business in the area will be looking for equipment and space. Consider supply sources from two different parts of the country, one close by and one several states away. (See checklist 7.)

Many disaster response plans focus on the total loss of equipment or buildings. This is the least common disaster. A better use of the disaster response team's time and energy is to look at the types of loss your institution typically experiences: interruptions of power and telecommunications; hardware breakdown; or computer network crashes. Focus your disaster response plan on these smaller-scale disasters. Prioritize your vulnerabilities to prevent or forestall the loss of data, equipment, and software. Part of the planning process entails thinking about what will happen if you lose various types of services.

Speculate on the types of damage you will sustain with each type of computer network loss. Discuss what the impact of the interruptions will be on services. Then write the response procedures so that the steps focus on the best processes to restore access to computers and their associated services.

Emotional Issues

No matter what the scale of the disaster, there is always some emotional stress. If the disaster is localized, then the stress on the computer disaster-response team members is usually from the extra workload. If there is a larger-scale disaster, such as loss of all the data and hardware, then the staff will have more emotional issues to deal with on top of the strain of restoring computer services to the entire network or institution. The staff who lose their data will also have to deal with issues such as the need to reconstruct data that wasn't captured during network or local backups. Limit the number of hours each disaster response team member can work to eight or ten hours. One way to deal with the extra workload is to divide the team into two or three groups so that each can work for a limited period of time on a problem and then the next group can approach the problem with fresh minds and perspectives. Working disaster response team members to exhaustion is not a productive use of their time, and will not get computer services restored any faster.

During a disaster there is an enormous amount of internal stress and guilt that manifests itself. Counseling should be included in all disaster response plans to help all staff deal with emotional stress and issues that revolve around crises. Set up a group meeting with counselors soon after the disaster occurs, say within 24–48 hours. Provide individual counseling to those who need more time to work through their own issues.

Coordinating Resources

When you design your disaster response plan, you need to consider the impact of loss of operations on four major aspects of your institution: people, communications, operations, and financial.[1] Each aspect has an important part to play in the operation and survival of any organiza-

tion. Although libraries, archives, and museums may have a longer recovery window, in today's fast-paced information-dependent society, any interruption in services means that your users and patrons will turn to new information resources and you will lose clientele.

Staff

When the disaster occurs, every person in each department is affected by the loss. Each person needs to have a role to play in the restoration of services, be it the computers, physical objects, or coordination of activities. In this way, your disaster response plan focuses emotional and physical energies in a positive way. As the staff work, the adrenaline works its way through their systems and dissipates the stress and emotions. You will need to build some flexibility into the roles of each staff member during a disaster. The wider the impact of the disaster, the more the personal lives of employees will be affected. Some may need to deal with family crises. This is another reason to stagger or rotate the disaster response team members in eight-hour shifts.

Disaster response team members may need to work off-site in the temporary location to restore computer operations. Others will work locally to recover what hardware can be salvaged. Still other non-disaster response team members will be assigned to help where needed in communications, various physical clean-up operations, and overall coordination of plans. Each person will also need time to relax and get away from the fast pace of disaster response operations.

Communications

One of the most essential parts of a disaster response plan is communications. In the case of computer disaster response plans there are four aspects to communications: internal; external— patrons, users, and the media; vendors; and computer telecommunications. Each level of the computer disaster response plan needs to build in ways to communicate in each of these areas. Let's take them one at a time.

Internal communications includes notifying the appropriate disaster response team members about the scope of the disaster, and informing individuals about where and when to report to begin recovery procedures. The disaster response team leaders need to keep their team members informed so they know when each set of procedures or priorities is completed. The disaster response team leaders also need to talk to each other and the administrators so that all plans can be somewhat coordinated and operations recovered in a timely manner. This will also enable administrators to discuss timelines for recovery with insurance companies, boards of trustees, and the media. Internal communications need to be active and frequent to keep everyone in the institution informed as to the status of the recovery operations.

External communications involves notifying those people who use your computer and information services that the systems are down and when operations will be restored. If there are alternative information service providers and resources that your users can access, give them that information. For instance, if the online catalog and electronic resources for the library/archive have crashed, let staff and users know if there is another library in the vicinity or in the consortium that can provide the access to those resources. If there is another library/archive branch in the area, move some of your staff to that area and provide services from that location. This is essential if a building is inaccessible for more than a day. Another option is to connect the mirror site to the main website and provide access to electronic services through your backup location. Let your various publics know about these alternative methods of access.

Another aspect of external communications is talking to the media. This is the trickiest aspect of communications because of the nature of mass media. Your disaster response plan must identify *one* spokesperson for the institution and that person will be the media contact, no matter what the size of the disaster. This media contact person may be the public information officer or the president of your institution. No matter whom you select, that person should be the only one discussing the status of the crisis with the media. The message delivered to the media should be positive and succinct. Describe the loss of computer and information services, the estimated time until everything is restored, and alternative methods of access and communications with the affected departments. If you need assistance with funding the recovery operations or with manpower, this is the time to ask for it.

Vendors and service providers need to know if there is a change in or loss of computer operations. You may have vendors and service providers who send orders through e-mail. If there is no response in your usual timely manner, they will go elsewhere.

Computer telecommunications involves having the computers talk to one another and to service providers. If you have fixed IP (Internet Protocol) addresses that are recognized by various service providers who license limited access to their commercial resources, you will need to let them know how the network and individual computers have been reconfigured so your staff and users can access information. Don't forget to build in a way for the various computer services team members to talk to each other, so that operations can be restored according to the pre-arranged priorities. You might want to assign an IT staff member to troubleshoot any unforeseen technology problems.

Operations or Services

When designing your disaster response plan, don't forget that all operations in your institution are interconnected. As you begin to look at prioritizing the restoration of services, your team members need to understand how the operations interconnect, and who can provide what services. Enlist the advice of the physical plant and maintenance staff when deciding if there is a good alternative location for restoring computer operations at your physical location. The planning team needs to decide what overall services can be temporarily outsourced or provided from remote locations. If information services can be provided via e-mail and chat rooms, then someone needs to build that into the disaster response plan. Teach the information services staff how to access the information from a remote location and the computer personnel how to configure external access to internal databases. Insert a work flow chart or organization chart in the appendix of your plan. Create a list of services and electronic resources per department, building, or network, along with the priority for restoration of those services. (See checklists 11 and 22–25.)

Financial

After communications, the most important aspect of a disaster response plan is determining who has the fiscal authority to issue an emergency purchase order, hire personnel, and rent space and equipment in an emergency. The disaster response team leaders need to know which administrator can purchase services and supplies. Determine who is authorized to declare a disaster and activate the insurance policy. Another issue for the disaster response team leaders to discuss with the administration is, how long can you work without an influx of money? If the institution charges users a fee for the use of its information or computers, how long can the services be unavailable before users seek another source? These financial factors will determine the order of restoration of all services within an institution and should be factored into the priorities for each level of the computer disaster response plan.

Another financial matter to determine during the planning phase is, how much will the insurance company pay and when? The institution may need to allocate emergency funds to pay for the purchase of new computer equipment and for temporary locations for computer operations. The disaster response team together with the fiscal services department need to determine how much money should be set aside for just these types of emergencies. (See checklist 12.)

As you design the various parts and pieces of your computer disaster response plan, the team needs to coordinate its priorities and financial needs with the institution's overall disaster response plan so there is no conflict of interest, time, and services when the entire institution faces a large-scale disaster response operation.

Locations for Providing Services

During the planning process, the disaster response teams need to delegate responsibility for what operations and services at which levels of the institution will be maintained and serviced by the various team members. Coordination and cooperation are the key. There must be agreement about the computational priorities of the institution and the library/archive. The types of services that may need to be restored include:

- administrative, human resources, financial, and other systems that affect the whole institution;
- services to the public (circulation and the online catalog), web and electronic resources, and various databases;
- inter- and intra-institutional methods of communication such as e-mail; and
- all other computer services.

When the disaster response team thinks about all the computer operations at the institution, its members need to ask some of the following questions of the library/archive staff.

Can the information service providers operate or provide public services from another building, another campus, or a remote location? If so, then the computer services department must arrange for the data to be mounted and available from the alternative site.

What about delivering information services from a remote location? Will it all be phone/e-mail and web-based? This is important if your organization's staff needs current and accurate information. The computer services department will need to make the necessary adjustments in its remote access programs to recognize authorized outside users.

What about the website and web-based services the institution provides? Are they housed, stored, or maintained locally? In the same building, on the same campus, the same town, or a remote location (best), and is there a mirror site? Design procedures in order to provide access to those web-based services within the allotted time frame. In this way, the library/archive can provide remote access.

Keeping Track of Your Resources

After thinking about protecting your software and data, you then have to create a list of what your department, building, system, and institution owns and uses, including hardware and software applications. (See checklists 5 and 6.) What are the basic components of each system? Does each have its own peripherals or do they share? Is each department using something different? As part of your computer disaster response plan, you need to document each computer system, its location, the server or network it is attached to, and the software and peripheral components, as well as the security protection installed. Diagram or document each computer in each room and arrange the information in the appendix of your plan for easy access. (See checklists 22, 23, and 24.) Append information about the priority for recovery, computer and department functions, and its place with the physical disaster response plan prioritization. Indicate the frequency of backup, where the data is stored remotely, and the person in charge of those pieces of computer equipment. Create a short checklist of the minimum functionality requirements for computer hardware and software for each system.

In creating your disaster response plan for computers, you have inventoried the hardware system configuration and network setups in each room of each building. At the same time you indicated the type of operating system, peripherals, and software applications on each network. Whenever there is a change to the configuration or the components of the computer network, you need to update your computer disaster response plan to reflect those changes.

Testing Restoration of Systems

Every disaster response plan needs to be tested. Just as the disaster response team for recovery of the physical collections tests its plans, so those who provide information and computer services must also test their plans. The staff who provide information services should practice working from remote locations off-site and in other buildings at the institution. Review the procedures for remote access to electronic resources, online catalogs, and websites as well as e-mail. (See checklist 3.) Make certain the instructions are clear and all staff can perform the necessary adjustments to their computer systems. This will be essential if information services are provided via e-mail or chat rooms.

The computer services department must test its backup procedures and data recovery operations. The computer disaster response plan should be tested at least once a year, if not every month. This means you should test that the team can identify what is wrong or lost, restore the entire system or parts of the system, and even replace all the hardware and peripherals. Don't forget to practice troubleshooting hardware and software compatibility problems. If you have to upgrade hardware or software to recover from a disaster, this will be a necessary procedure. You might want to involve the computer technical support staff in this part of testing your recovery plan.

Create a testing schedule for the team. For instance, you could test the backup equipment once a month, installation of parts of a backup once a month, installation of all software once a quarter, and configuration of all the hardware and software once a year. Be certain to document those procedures that don't work or must be modified; change the procedures in the manual right away and then test them in the next cycle. It would also be a good idea to have the alternate disaster response team members participate in the testing. Invite the members of the institution-wide computer disaster response team to participate, and ask to participate in their planning and exercises.

Provide training sessions for individual departments on how to perform simple backup routines on the stand-alone and networked computers. Show them how to perform simple recovery procedures, such as "undeleting" a deleted file. Simple written procedures are best.

Disaster Response Plan Components

The disaster response activation plan itself should be very short, say one page per building or department. The plan will consist of a number of sections. The shortest sections go in front. The activation plan will contain lists of contacts and basic procedures. (See checklist 9 for a sample disaster response plan.) Extensive checklists, protocols, and prioritization lists should follow the basic plan requirements in appendices. Make certain all the procedures are written in clear, concise steps. Follow the procedures your disaster response team created during the planning phase. If there are steps that don't work, indicate what they are and revise the plan afterward. Whatever you do, don't "wing it." Remember, the plan was created when everything was calm. When it's calm again, it's time to evaluate and make revisions.

To give one example, a disaster response or contingency plan to back up and restore data files contains the following elements:

- Contact information for all computer staff (local, building, and institution-wide)
- Gathering place to meet prior to assessing the damage and amount of loss of computer software and hardware
- Hot site, cold site firm contact name and number, along with who is authorized to declare a disaster. Append a map with directions.
- Remote operations location with name and number of contact person. Append a map with directions.
- Emergency contact information for all department heads and for other disaster response team leaders
- List of personnel responsible for backing up the data and software
- Frequency and type of backup for each computer and network system
- Storage location and contact information for 24-hour retrieval of backup tapes or files. Append map and directions.

- Contact name and numbers for remounting software and data files onto computers
- Contact name and numbers for fixing or replacing damaged hardware
- Contact information and/or preapproved purchase orders for emergency acquisition of computers (hardware and software)
- Contact information for all branch and department heads
- Priority or order for restoring computer services per building and department
- Simple written procedures for reconfiguring hardware, and remounting and reinstalling software
- Diagrams that show which computers are associated with which networks and peripheral equipment
- Inventory of hardware and software by room or department, including serial numbers for hardware, serial numbers and licenses for all software, location of any printed manuals
- Insurance contact person and amount of deductible for computers and rental of space
- Team member to document loss; written inventory and visual descriptions of loss for insurance claim
- Contact information for communications contact person to deal with the media
- Emergency contacts for restoring power, phones, and telecommunications or to switch service as needed to alternative location
- Contact information for statewide and regional consortia

NOTE

1. Jeffrey W. Greenberg, "September 11, 2001: A CEO's Story," *Harvard Business Review* (October 2002): 4.

5
Disaster Response

*When Everything
Goes Wrong*

I t's unexpected, that call out of the blue that comes in the night or when it's most inconvenient. The frantic call that says the computers aren't working. All that hard work of practicing loading backup data and reconfiguring computer hardware now comes rushing to the fore. If you have planned and prepared, your reactions will be automatic. Grab your plan, call your disaster response team, and get the response and recovery effort under way. In the computer side of disaster response, every second counts. (See checklist 1 for a sample step-by-step action plan.)

Gather Your Disaster Response Team

When you activate your disaster response plan, the first step is to get the team in one place so that you can determine how much damage there is and what your priorities for recovery will be. The disaster response team leaders need to coordinate their actions, so that resources are used where they are needed first. If the team is spread out geographically, get the local members together while keeping in contact with the others. Be prepared to declare a disaster based upon your initial assessment of the damage. Alert the hot site, mobile recovery site, or the remote site of the potential for a disaster declaration.

Don't forget to see what the other disaster response teams in your institution are doing in terms of response. Those staff members who have to deal with the physical collections will also need to be coordinating access to the building. Remember, you have to work in a coordinated manner to get all the operations back up and running in a timely manner.

Assess the Damage

Your ability to assess the damage is dependent upon access to the buildings where the computer networks are housed. If you cannot get into the buildings, then you will need to "declare a disaster" and get the disaster response team to the hot site or remote location in order to get the backup software applications and data up and running. Do not delay on this issue.

If you can get into the building, assess what is damaged. Has the building suffered a loss of power and telecommunications? Did the outage result in damaged hardware or a loss of data?

Estimate the time until you will gain access to the building, the data, the power, and equipment. If this is longer than your institution is able to tolerate, then you will need to declare a disaster and activate your data recovery plan.

Assess the scope of the damage. How much is not usable: the room, floor, building, the entire institution?

Alert your insurance company as to the scope and amount of damage. Activate your business resumption and computer insurance policies.

Once you assess the scope of damage and duration of outages, you will need to begin recovery operations. Review priorities for resumption of services and coordinate recovery with the other disaster response teams.

Begin Recovery Operations

Once you have determined the type and scope of damage, provide the disaster response team members with information about which software applications and data to install on the remote systems. If you are going to be reloading the data locally, get those operations started.

Determine the amount of lost or permanently damaged equipment and order replacements from the approved computer vendors. Order computer peripherals as needed.

Notify the remote operations person to begin operations from the remote facility or hot site. Have the necessary computer components and office equipment delivered to this temporary location. Begin installation of hardware; get the networks reconfigured physically, wired for telecommunication, and then installed with the appropriate operating systems, software applications, and data. (Your disaster response team should have practiced all these procedures during the testing phase of your disaster response plan process.)

During the response and recovery phase of the disaster, the disaster response team leaders should meet twice daily in the beginning, if not more often, to coordinate their activities and update where the teams are in their plans. Meet with the team members at the beginning and end of each shift in order to make certain that all the recovery actions are staying coordinated and everyone knows what is to be accomplished next. Keep the administrators apprised, on a regular basis, of progress in restoration of computer and information services.

6

Disaster Response Planning for Hardware and Physical Storage Media

We have looked at the team players and their responsibilities and how to activate your disaster response plan for data recovery. Now let's look at the hardware and physical storage medium side of a disaster response plan. Although this book is concentrated on the software and data side of disaster response, we have to include plans to recover or replace hardware. While working on this part of your response plan, consider how you would streamline computer hardware if you had to replace it all.

One of the most important things to remember is just because equipment is wet doesn't mean that it is destroyed. Now, if the computers were running and they became inundated by water, then the equipment is probably dead. But if they are off and become wet with clean water, then you should be able to dry them, clean them, and have them recertified.

Two things you should *not* do are turn the computers on when they are wet, and try to use them when they are dirty (with debris from ceiling tiles, airborne dust from the outside, or soot from a fire). Trying to salvage the physical computers depends upon the type of damage that has been sustained. If the computers are floating in water, make certain the electricity is off, then remove the cables from the back, pick the computers up, open their covers, and let the water drain out. Then you'll have to decide if the computers are worth saving or if it would be less expensive to simply replace them. Your organization's ability to replace computers may also depend upon the type and amount of computer insurance carried. (See also case study 2 at the end of this chapter.)

There are two ways to protect your hardware: keep it from sustaining physical damage from use, abuse, and the environment; and upgrade it enough to prevent obsolescence. In the first case, you want to place hardware in locations that are not prone to leaks, excess dust, soot, and debris. You also want to make certain the furniture that supports the hardware is stable and strong enough to hold the weight. Don't place computer components on the floor where they can be knocked over or get wet. Of course, you also want good surge protectors and uninterruptible power supplies for each set of computer components. All this is common sense.

Activating the Plan

Assessing the Physical Damage

First, as with disaster response plans for physical collections, the computer disaster response team needs to determine the extent of the damage. What type of disaster occurred? Is it water, fire, debris, or electrical damage? Were the computers on when the disaster occurred? Can you get access to them and remove the equipment from the area while general cleanup takes place? If you cannot remove the computer equipment and cannot treat it immediately, then decrease the humidity, increase the air flow, and cover the equipment to protect it from additional airborne debris. Identify where the backup diskettes, CDs, and tapes are stored. Are the backup tapes stored next to the computers, near them, or somewhere else? Are the backups also damaged, wet, melted, or dirty?

Implementing Physical Recovery Procedures

Once you have determined the type and scope of damage, then you will need to decide if the area where the hardware is located will be accessible quickly or if you need to set up computer operations in a separate location. If you can get into the location and it can be usable in the next few hours, then evaluate the damage to the hardware to see if it can be dried, cleaned, and recertified or if the equipment is so damaged it must be replaced. Order any replacements based upon the inventory taken prior to the disaster, so that the equipment performs the same functions. That's all a typical insurance rider for computers will cover.

If you cannot get access to the building or computers, then activate your computer disaster response plan and get the necessary computer staff together at that remote location to activate the plan, install everything needed, and provide access from afar.

Insurance

Insurance policies are an essential part of any disaster response plan and associated loss prevention. When reviewing your disaster response plan, you need two separate riders: computer insurance to cover computers, and business resumption insurance to cover operating from a remote location.

Computer Insurance Riders

While designing the hardware part of your disaster response plan, you need to evaluate the insurance rider that covers computers to see what its limitations are. The computer rider is separate from the insurance that you purchase with your data storage company for hot, cold, and mobile sites. Basic computer riders start with coverage for the hardware in your computer system. The rider covers loss of hardware and loss of the location from which to run the computers. The policy covers purchasing new computers, and cleaning and reconditioning those computers that can be saved after a fire, flood, or loss of the building envelope. Computer insurance policies also pay for a specific amount of time in a rented location with rented equipment —at a hot, cold, or mobile recovery site—usually for two to three months, depending on the type of loss. Of course, if you pay for more insurance, it may cover you for longer or for more items. Most computer riders cover the purchase of hardware that will perform the same functions as those you lost.

No computer policy covers the reconstruction of data. Insurance companies assume that if there are computers, then those responsible are backing up their data and know how to re-create the computer system and network. Unlike the business resumption insurance rider which pays for reconstructing a paper inventory, the computer rider never pays for reconstruction of data. Depending on the type of computers and data your organization has, and the value of that data to your patrons, you will want to look into data insurance as well as business interruption insurance.[1]

Business Interruption or Resumption Insurance

Business resumption insurance is used to cover the rental of a temporary office or building, to hire temporary staff, rent or lease equipment and furniture, and pay salaries or unemployment fees. This insurance rider also pays to reconstruct a paper inventory, but not any computer data. The business resumption insurance pays to recondition other types of office equipment such as photocopiers. The duration of coverage and monthly expenditures will be determined at the time you purchase this insurance. Traditionally, business interruption policies are effective for a maximum of twelve months, at which time the insurance company assumes you will have gained access to your building or will have a new location to operate from.

Your insurance policy should be reviewed every three years; when you add departments; increase the amount of computer equipment; increase or decrease your fiscal needs; or when something else major changes.[2] (See checklist 12 when planning for business resumption insurance.)

When evaluating your insurance coverage, note the deductibles so that the disaster response team and library/archive administration are aware of how much they will need to spend before the insurance policy kicks in. This is the time to consider where the library/archive will find emergency funds to operate or replace equipment and collections.

Physical Recovery of Storage Media

Next we turn to the physical recovery of storage media: diskettes, CDs, and tapes.[3] If they have become wet, the best thing to do is to remove them from the water and get them dried off. *Do not* let the storage media dry by themselves or they will stick together and you will lose everything.

Magnetic Tape

Magnetic tape is the same or similar in composition to audio tape and other types of audiovisual storage materials. There is a base, usually polyester or some other inert plastic; an emulsion that is soft and holds the magnetic particles; and a binder that glues the emulsion to the base. The emulsion will stick to the base or any other surface when wet. If allowed to dry while touching something else, the emulsion will peel off and be lost forever. In addition, it is important to check that the tape is wound properly and tightly on the spool. If there are gaps in the tape, then debris can get trapped within and requires more handling to dry and clean the surfaces. To treat immediately, first rinse the tapes in distilled water, carefully wipe with a damp cloth, repeat, then carefully wipe dry with a clean lint-free cloth. Cassettes should be stood on the short end to dry. Wound tape should be hung by the center ring or hub. If the tapes must wait for treatment, then immerse them in cool distilled water until there is time to treat the tapes. There is equipment that you can rent or purchase that dries and cleans magnetic tape. When you are done cleaning the tape, inspect the contents to confirm that all the data is present. You may wish to copy or transfer the data to a new tape, and you should again confirm that all the data is readable. If possible, do all the copying and inspecting on an external drive that can be cleaned when the recovery project is over.

There are companies that sell magnetic tape-cleaning devices that clean and inspect dirty magnetic tape (including computer, audio, and video tapes).[4] These commercially available devices remove dirt and dust particles from the surface of the tape and inspect it for damage. These devices should be used if there is a fire, flooding, or construction in your building or the area where the magnetic media are stored. If you do store your backup data on-site, then this should be a short-term storage solution only. A rule of thumb might be one week. After that, the storage media should be transferred to a remote location. You should have distinct sets of backup data, not just overwritten diskettes and tapes.

Optical Discs

For compact discs, laser discs, DVDs, and other forms of optical disc, remove them from the water. Make certain that water is not trapped inside the disc itself, and put the discs in a dish drain to dry. If the water was dirty, then carefully rinse the discs using a soft sponge dipped in soapy water. Do not rub the surface. When dry, clean the discs using a dry, lint-free cloth and moving in a manner perpendicular to the grooves. Do not clean in a circular manner or you will scratch the surface. Do not spray the surface of compact discs with any cleaners. Spray the cloth instead.

Diskettes

Remove a diskette carefully from its container by slowly prying the metal door open, and then pop the case open. Let the diskette dry. Do not crimp or bend the magnetic medium inside. If the water was dirty, then carefully rinse the diskette using a soft sponge dipped in soapy water. Do not rub the surface. Once dry, clean very carefully with a lint-free cloth, put into a new diskette case (you don't need the metal door), copy onto a new diskette, and discard the original. You might not want to use your newest computers to do this copying. You'll also need to clean the disk drive when you are done with all this copying. It might be easier to use an external disk drive.

Directions and illustrations for cleaning physical storage media can be found in Joe Iraci, *Disaster Recovery of Modern Information Carriers: Compact Discs, Magnetic Tapes, and Magnetic Disks;* and Miriam Kahn, *Disaster Response and Prevention for Computers and Data*. (See note 3 below.)

NOTES

1. Kevin Savetz, "Data Insurance—Cover Your Most Valuable Assets—The Intangible Ones," *New Architect* (May 2002), www.newarchitectmag.com/documents/ s=2450/new1017879012973/index.html.
2. Charlie Kuyk, "Resolving Business Interruption Claims," *Columbus C.E.O.* (March 2002): 39–40.
3. Directions and illustrations for cleaning magnetic media can be found in Joe Iraci, *Disaster Recovery of Modern Information Carriers: Compact Discs, Magnetic Tapes, and Magnetic Disks,* Technical Bulletin no. 25 (Ottawa, Ont.: Canadian Conservation Institute, Department of Canadian Heritage, 2002); and Miriam Kahn, *Disaster Response and Prevention for Computers and Data* (Columbus, Ohio: MBK Consulting, 1994).
4. RTI Group sells equipment for cleaning magnetic media of all types, including magnetic reel tapes and video and audio cassettes; see www.rtico.com/ cw8000.html. It also sells machines for checking and cleaning compact discs of all types; see www.rtico. com/discchek/index.html.

CASE STUDY TWO

Water Damage and Computerized Public Records

It's the middle of the afternoon when the records center is at its busiest, accepting legal documents for filing, scanning and indexing the data, and helping the multitude of patrons. All of a sudden there is a bang, the sprinkler head over the main desk explodes, and water spurts everywhere. As fire alarms ring and security evacuates the building, the first thing going through your head is, "How much is lost? And how fast can we be back in operation?" Within five minutes water soaks three computers, the towers that were on the floor, desk drawers, the entire carpeted floor, and any legal documents on the desks. Then the water runs down the walls and into the office below. Once the water is shut off and it stops raining into the records center, the staff is allowed to enter the building and their offices. What a mess!

There is an inch or so of standing water everywhere, in desk drawers and on the floor. Fortunately, the sprinkler head exploded during the daytime, when there was staff in the building to shut off the water. As the staff return to the records center, they begin to assess the damage. There are wet computers, wet carpets, and wet documents. The director of the records center decides to close the office until everything is cleaned up.

(Cont'd)

Water Damage and Computerized Public Records *(Cont'd)*

The three computers that are wet were on and were standing in water. The towers are a total loss as are the monitors, so the director calls the computer vendor they leased from to come and replace the equipment. The wet legal documents are boxed up. Because the documents had not yet been recorded, security for the documents is required, and freeze-drying is the preferred method. These items are shipped for drying immediately and are returned within a week or so. Next the standing water is removed and the carpets are dried. The sprinkler head is replaced and the system is checked for leaks and breaks. Fortunately the older records are dry. By the next day the records center is open for operations. Once the documents have been returned, the records center has to record, index, and make available all those documents. To handle this backlog of work, the office hires temporary staff to input data and scan the documents. Within a month, the backlog is gone and normal operations have resumed. Without temporary help, it would have taken several extra weeks to process the documents on top of the regular workload.

Fortunately, the records center doesn't house the server or the backups for the images of documents. Even more fortunate, the computer equipment for scanning the new documents was far away from the broken sprinkler head, so that equipment was undamaged. The only thing lost was time and that day's work.

Usually the images are backed up onto microfilm daily at the archives, a physically separate building down the road. The microfilm is the legal surrogate and preferred method of preservation and long-term retention. The scanned images are burned onto optical discs and then sent to the computer vendor electronically, where they are mounted on servers at the vendor's headquarters in another state.

This particular records center had no disaster response plan, but it does have an excellent service contract with the computer vendor. This company leases the computer equipment to its clients. The company services the equipment and repairs or replaces damaged components. Software and equipment are upgraded on a regular basis as part of the contract. In this way the records center pays to lease the equipment but doesn't have to buy into upgrading on a regular basis. As improvements are made to the system, the clients' equipment and software are upgraded. That's all part of the contract. The computer vendor mounts each client's data onto a national database which the vendor maintains. Backups of the national database are performed regularly, daily at the minimum. The contractor will also provide microfilm and scanned image backup discs for its clients on a contractual basis.

Even though the records center had no disaster response plan, it was back in operation within twelve hours. There was only that day's data lost. Access to existing data was still available through the Internet, although it could not be accessed locally that particular day. Because of the multiple sites for backup data, all prior scanned images were safe and accessible via the World Wide Web. Even if the records center had been flooded during the night, the records had been microfilmed as required by state law. Access to the documents would have been slower, but possible due to preservation planning efforts in the past. Operations could have been moved to the archives or another government facility on a temporary basis. All in all, the records center made a successful recovery from an unexpected crisis.

SECTION TWO

Now that we have looked at protecting data from loss in the short term, let's turn our attention to long-term retention issues.

The mandate for "archiving" or preserving digital materials often comes from the top and even if it does not, it must be supported by the top administrators within the organization and should embrace the needs of users at all levels of the organization. As the library or archive as a whole embarks on digital projects—including the digitization of printed materials and the original creation of digital documents, databases, and websites—you must decide during this planning process about how to store, keep, maintain, and update any and all digital materials. There are a number of information technology disciplines at work on long-term storage and retention programs for digital materials. The financial, legal, travel, library and archive, and records management fields are all concerned about current-day storage and recovery of data. The library/archive and records management fields seem to be the ones most concerned about retrieving data and documents created long ago, however. The financial and legal industries are concerned about legal issues involving the retention of records for the legally mandated time, and appropriate destruction afterwards. In the aftermath of the Enron and other corporate scandals, the public has become aware that businesses don't always keep their e-mail and documents forever or even as long as they should legally, and the cost to retrieve unindexed data can be prohibitive.

Libraries and archives, individually and through overarching national organizations, are looking at issues of long-term retention of digital resources at both the local and national levels. What are long-term storage and retention issues, and how can libraries and archives plan for them? And will the data be accessible in the future? Some granting agencies are also concerned with these issues, because electronic resources and digital libraries are being created using public funds, but the institutions involved are not necessarily planning on how to preserve or archive the digital resources when funding ceases.

So what's the difference between digital libraries and digital archives? Digital libraries are collections of electronic resources, digital images and texts, databases, and catalogs. Their materials may or may not be unique. By contrast, a digital archive is a collection of digital documents and materials that are stored for the long term with access points and descriptions of provenance. The expectation for digital archives is that the electronic materials will be available well into the future. That means that accessibility will continue regardless of the software that created the data, usually in nonproprietary formats. The data will be moved from one storage format to another as time and needs warrant. Digital libraries may be accessed by anyone, while access to digital archives may be limited depending upon their contents and the creating agency.

There is an obvious conflict between burning CDs for "archival purposes" and the rapid obsolescence of hardware, software, and operating systems that negates this "archival" treatment for purposes of long-term retention. This catch-22 is a serious issue! Technology is being used to preserve the data, yet the data cannot be read without the preservation of compatible technology.

There is a misperception today among the general public that saving or burning an item on a CD-ROM, DVD, or even a diskette or tape backup means that the data is "preserved." Just watch advertisements on the television. One commercial shows a couple transferring all their videos to DVD to preserve them forever and then throwing the tapes out the window. The electronics industry, not necessarily the customer, is driving this cyclical migration from one format to another.

Another example of planned obsolescence is found in a recent article in *CNET News.com*, which announced that Dell is planning to discontinue floppy drives in all its laptops and in Dimension Dell desktops, just as Apple's new iMac doesn't have a floppy drive.[1] (Hewlett-Packard and eMachines are also planning this change in design.) They plan instead to offer "flash memory," which is a small portable data storage device (about half the size of a fountain pen) that will hold up to four gigabytes of memory. Flash memory plugs into your USB port. You just copy the files from your hard drive to the flash memory, the same as you would to a diskette or CD-ROM. But what will institutions and individuals do when they want to retrieve data from their floppy discs? Or their CDs?

There are many professionals in the library/ archive field who feel that using a "standard" digital format such as JPEG or GIF for an image means that the image will always "be there" and be readily accessible by new technologies. Others feel that TIFF (Tagged Image File Format) may be the better digital format because it is not compressed and is more universally readable. However, TIFF images take up a lot of space and memory, perhaps more than your institution can afford.

Another perceived standard applies to text, databases, and data, where ASCII is the most universal format for characters in text files. There are many people who save their files in Microsoft Word formats (by far the most prominent word-processing software today), and PDF (Portable Document Format) is also becoming a standard data presentation format. Although Adobe's PDF format is proprietary, the company seems to be making a long-term commitment to maintain PDF compatibility and accessibility to all with free viewer software. There is no standard text format today, but "best practices" documents show that the simpler and more universal the text format, the better the chances for eventual deciphering and retrieval of the data by new technologies.

Digital projects that emphasize "preserving" our heritage or documents must plan for the future by the copying and reformatting of data, images, and indexes to new storage media. Scanning the item and then making the digital image available to the public are only part of the "archival" or long-term storage issue in the context of a continuing information revolution.

Some of the questions being asked of digital data and its creators are: how are you going to store it? Where? Will the data be readable next year? Two years from now? How far into the future are you thinking? What happens if the server crashes this week and you don't have a tape backup? Then what? Who will you call to reconstruct the data, and what if it's classified or of a sensitive nature? What if your hardware or software system hasn't been upgraded for a number of years or is no longer being made? Then what will you do? What if it's the leading edge of technology and no "techie" in your institution, town, or state has worked on that piece of equipment yet and the manufacturer has just upgraded the hardware to something newer?

These are serious questions to consider when looking at long-term retention plans for digital materials. Another question to ask is: what good is storing the data if you cannot access specific pieces of data? Backup tapes are perfect for short-term storage and prevention of total loss due to a disaster. The data is stored sequentially and can be reinstalled onto a computer with relative ease in exactly the same order. So this is good for disaster prevention, but not for long-term access, because the backup tape data is completely unindexed. Archiving your data for long-term retention must include creating access points using indexing, metadata tagging, XML, or some other method of identifying specific data elements or files.

Public record centers seem to be thinking a little ahead on this question. They digitize materials for public use and access either in-house or over the Web, then create a preservation or archival copy of microfilm from the digital images, using one of several technologies. Essentially,

the microfilm is generated by computer from the digital images in staggered copy streams, not necessarily in one continuous copy stream. Ideally, the physical storage media for the digital images and the microfilm should be stored in separate locations in environmentally controlled storage areas. Some organizations store their backups (tape, discs, microfilm) at their service provider, some at record storage centers, others at places like Iron Mountain or UMI that have vast underground storage areas under strict environmental control.

In just the same way, libraries and archives that embark on digital projects need to plan for the future as they design today's digital projects. The chapters in section 2 will discuss:

- what questions to ask (chapter 7, protecting data)
- what decisions to consider and criteria to use; and where to look for answers (chapter 8, decision making)
- which organizations are looking at long-term retention "best practices" for digital materials (chapter 9, the future)

By planning up front for long-term access to and retention of digital materials, we ensure that they will last for many years to come.

NOTE

1. John G. Spooner, "Dell Foments Floppy's Fall," *CNET News.com* (February 6, 2003), http://news.com.com/ 2100-1040-983596.html.

7
Protecting Data for Long-Term Retention

Digital storage is easy; digital preservation is hard. Preservation means keeping the stored information cataloged, accessible, and usable on current media, which requires constant effort and expense. —Stewart Brand

Designing the Project

Mission Policies and Users

The mission of librarians, archivists, and records managers for years to come will be to protect data so that it exists as far into the future as possible, and is accessible to anyone who wishes to access the materials. Nowadays, in addition to preserving the physical object, we must preserve the intellectual content of our digital projects and documents. We will be better prepared to protect our data if we ask certain questions while we are creating the digital materials.

As with many projects, we need to keep in mind key factors about our institutions and their patrons or users. (See also checklist 26.) Those factors are:

- the underlying mission of the institution and of the library or archive collections;
- the collecting policy; and
- the patrons' or users' needs.

With these general questions in mind, you need to explore whether any other institution is considering the same digital project. The most important issue to explore is the state of your internal resources (time, funds, personnel, and technical expertise). There needs to be a solid, long-term commitment from the administrators to continue funding of the project, not just its creation but its continued existence.

Let's approach these factors as a whole.

The mission of your institution and its library, archive, or museum should be foremost in your mind when contemplating any project. It is the reason for your organization's existence. If you serve the general public and their reading needs or perhaps their local history and genealogy research needs, then the types of projects you create should fill those needs. If your organization is an academic institution, then you serve the faculty and students by supporting their curricula as well as their scientific and research pursuits. Museum libraries and archives serve the curators and exhibition staff, providing for their research needs. Archives hold the records of their institutions as well as historical papers relating to their mission. Special and business libraries serve their own internal clientele. The needs of all these publics are different. The scope of collecting policies will vary with the size, depth, and wealth of the institution.

The audience for the project is probably the most difficult to determine, especially given the wide reach of the World Wide Web. One academic consortium mounted full-text databases of nineteenth-century books and journals dealing with the Reconstruction period, some fairly obscure, and of particular interest to historians of that time period. After making the images available on the Web, they found that genealogists and family historians were their heaviest users, in addition to their faculty, especially when they added collections with information about the Civil War.[1]

Resources

After you review your institution's mission, its collecting policies, and the needs of your users, you need to look at the resources available at your institution and library or archive. There has to be a serious commitment not just to support the project, because it is the current trend to create digital projects, but to continue caring for the data and associated programs long after it stops being "the thing" to fund. There should be discussion and an approach created during the planning phase of a digitization project that considers what happens to the project when the seed money or grant money runs out, how your institution or department is going to fund storage and continued access to the collection of data and digital materials, and for how long.

Accessing Information

There are several interconnected elements to supporting a digital project, just as there were when we funded microfilming projects. Support consists of providing our institution with its most precious resources: time, personnel, and money. The least expensive part of the support is the equipment. It is basically a one-time investment (although you will have to purchase upgrades in hardware and software applications). But once you buy the equipment, you have to staff it.

Staffing the equipment and the project is the most expensive part of the equation, because you have to find ongoing funds to do this. The cost of staff includes their pay, benefits, and the continuing training required to develop, create, and maintain the digital project for many years into the future. Just look at microfilming equipment that is gathering dust in your storage rooms. After the initial funding, there wasn't enough staff or money to continue the project for which the equipment was purchased.

The last type of support includes providing the assigned staff enough time each day or week or month to work on the project, especially after its initial creation. This commitment to long-term support is extremely important for grant-funded projects. The granting agency often pays the initial project costs, but not the upkeep and maintenance. Creating a project only to let it linger a long death doesn't serve our users' needs.

After deciding to pursue the digital project, you need to think about the design of the project. Digitization is all the rage right now, but how will your users access the data? You need to think about all the interconnecting issues before you spend any of your resources (time, staff, and money) on the project. The interconnecting issues include the software applications you will use to create the data; the access and searching methods people will use to find the data; description and subject headings for the data; and the method you will use to track changes to the data and its associated structure. You don't want to digitize a huge amount of materials only to find that no one knows what's on the CDs and there is no search mechanism to find the desired data. Think about all the newspapers that are microfilmed that have no indices. Patrons have to scroll through entire runs looking for an obituary or event unless they know the specific date. Isn't this one of the reasons we dislike microfilm? So why create digital materials with the same lack of access points? If you contract out the creation of the digital project, you need to outline and describe all the access points and descriptions before you find a vendor to do the work for you. (See case study 3 at the end of this chapter.)

When selecting the software applications to use to create your data, consider using something nonproprietary. Nonproprietary software applications are not dependent upon a specific operating system, application, or computing platform. They will create the data in simple, plain, fairly universal formats as opposed to proprietary formats. If you cannot find a nonproprietary software application, use software that "everyone else" is using. There is strength in numbers. If commercial software is being widely used and adapted by cultural institutions, then buy into that product. The more people using the product, the better chance we have of that company creating future- and backward-compatible versions of the software. Encrypted, password-protected, and copyright-protected data is much harder to access as time goes on than data that is stored in simple formats. Consider storing the long-term version and its associated metadata in simple text files.

When evaluating software applications and data structure, you will want to consider how to add more data, images, or fields in subsequent phases, over a period of years. Selecting a widely used program will help you ensure that newly created electronic data will be compatible with the original software application.[2]

In the creation of digital objects, you need to document where the data or images came from, how they are interconnected, and what criteria you used to include or exclude items. (See checklists 27 and 28.) This documentation is the metadata, or part of it, and it will be essential for future generations to understand the structure of your data files. You might document how the access points were created and how the search mechanism works. If you used a thesaurus to provide standard subject headings, put that into your document. You will also want to document what software applications you used to create the digital objects originally. Put this information into simple "read-me" text files that will be carried into the future along with their associated data objects.

Take time to think about the access points and descriptions for each piece of data that you will want. Don't just think about how you would describe the data, but consider how your users would search for it. Don't limit your searching ability. You will want the ability to search on more than one subject heading, as well as the title, creator, and accession or call number. You need to think seriously about your file and image naming conventions before you name the first file. Will you be able to identify the digital file by its name alone? Make certain you document your naming protocol in the "read-me" file.

When you plan the long-term retention of digital materials, you must think about how you will access the data in the future. "Possibly most important is the recognition that archiving must be considered at the time the material is created rather than at the end of the distribution chain."[3]

Digital project designers are now using XML (Extensible Markup Language) to create metadata or information about files, images, websites, and much more. XML is a nonproprietary system that is based on SGML (Standard Generalized Markup Language). It is a set of universal rules designed to describe data and documents in digital format. XML provides elements that identify distinct portions of data within a digital document. The elements are embedded the same way HTML tags are embedded within a web page. The markup tags can also identify attributes of the digital document. XML is an open standard maintained by the World Wide Web Consortium (W3C). XML is also designed to enable the portability of files across the Web and across various platforms and information sources.[4]

After deciding what to create and how to access that data within the digital files, you need to think about the long-term issues of protecting the physical and intellectual data. Of course, there are now new questions to ask. Who will be responsible for the all-important future plans, copying, migration, and reformatting of the data and software to new hardware and software systems? Your organization or a vendor will have to do the work. How will you allocate staff time and funding? Will you insist that the staff assigned do the work in their "spare time," or will you create a position that is responsible for the long-term care and handling of all digital collections? Or will your organization contract out the service? It is possible that a contractor could provide this copying and migration service at a much lower cost than your institution could do itself, and could also do the work using preprogrammed robotic processes. If this is the case, then everyone wins as long as the contractor is in business.

Planning the Project

Planning for the Future

The institution-wide computer staff is responsible for maintaining hardware and software and responding to disasters. Are they also responsible for grading the software and hardware for the digital project? Maybe not. Perhaps this is the responsibility of the data project creators or webmasters? Of course, these data creators should be communicating with the institution-wide computing center staff, letting them know how the software applications and data structures have changed. This should trigger new backup routines, particularly if the new databases or systems are critical to the smooth running of the library or archive. Each change should be documented in the computer disaster response plan at local, network, and institution-wide levels. Who in the various computer departments gets training on the new equipment and software applications? The future of your data is dependent upon staff being able to keep up with changes in all aspects of technology. So the plan for long-term retention requires the allocation of funds for training of computer staff and department liaisons.

Planning for the future of your digital collections is essential at the point when you embark on digital projects, be they the creation of digital libraries and collections or the scanning of physical documents or electronic resources.

Procedures and Protocols

During the planning phase, discuss the procedures and protocols for protecting the data and for accessing and storing the digital material objects (i.e., data and storage media) into the future. The only way to ensure the data will be there is to be proactive. This is the most cost-effective approach to the long-term retention of digital materials. All timetables should be thought out, resources allocated, and funding sources considered during the planning phase of any digital project. Of course, no one knows what the future holds in the computing field. We only know it is a swiftly moving target with which we have to keep pace.

Planning Questions

When the planning phase for creating the data, images, and digital resources of your long-term

digital project is complete, document the decisions you have made. These decisions should include:

> How will the digital resources be kept for future access and use?
>
> Who will be responsible for "revisiting" the issues of backup, funding, and preservation in the future?
>
> Who will fund all future management of the data?
>
> How often will you plan to revisit these issues?

Consider these questions carefully and schedule a review of resource allocation regularly with administrators and digital resources creators. Conducting a review every fiscal cycle seems to be too often and too short-sighted, while scheduling it every five years seems too long.

NOTES

The epigraph for this chapter is a quote from Stewart Brand, "Ending the Digital Dark Age," in *The Clock of the Long Now: Time and Responsibility—the Ideas behind the World's Slowest Computer* (New York: Basic, 1999), 88.

1. Making of America is a joint project of Cornell University and the University of Michigan and is at http://moa.umdl.umich.edu/.
2. The National Archives and Records Administration (NARA) has established protocols for the transfer from government agencies to NARA of electronic records for long-term storage and retention as described in NARA's "Electronic Records Management Manual" at www.archives.gov/about_ us/ regulations/part_1228_1.html. There is additional information in the Electronic Records Archives section of the NARA site, www.archives.gov/electronic_ records_archives/index.html.
3. Deanna Marcum and Amy Friedlander, "Keepers of the Crumbling Culture: What Digital Preservation Can Learn from Library History," *D-Lib Magazine* 9, no. 5 (May 2003): 6; www.dlib.org/dlib/may03/friedlander/ 05friedlander.html.
4. Definition of XML found at W3C website, www.w3c. org/XML/.

CASE STUDY THREE

Think of Access When You Digitize

Digitizing is all the rage, so your director decides that the pictures and photographs in the vertical file should be digitized so all the genealogists can use them. "That's great," you say, "but what about the news and article clippings?" After getting the go-ahead, you hire a student from the art college to start digitizing the contents of the vertical file. Wow! That went really quickly and smoothly; the student was a whiz at scanning.

Now comes the real test: a researcher comes in to find pictures of 100-year-old houses in your community. "Wait a minute and I'll pull up digital images of the houses," you reply. Off you go to put in the CDs of the pictures and find the one that has houses on it. But when you look at the file names, all you see are numbers. There are no subject files and no discernible names. After trying a few files, you give up and go looking for the vertical files. The vertical files are packed away in boxes in the back room next to the scanner. The items are completely out of order and the student has gone back to school. Now what? What happened to the great digital project that was supposed to help the library and the librarians save time? You look at the researcher and suggest they return in a few weeks when the vertical files are back in order.

What happened? What do you do now? What happened is that no one thought about how the digital images were going to be retrieved or used. The director gave you money for this project, and you gave someone the task of making the image files. That was that, but it wasn't enough. It was easy to create the images. After all, it's just like the photos you take with a camera when you order a disc instead of physical pictures. You get a disc with file numbers but no identifying information. You have to sort through them and decide how to identify and find the images later. So too with your vertical file. It was your job and that of your colleagues to think about how the images would be accessed. The least you could have done was instruct the student to scan each image into a file with the subject heading from the vertical file. Then you could have scrolled through each image in that file on the CD. But isn't that just like the hunt through the vertical file itself? Computers are more powerful, after all, and we should be using the computer more thoroughly. Lack of planning on your part resulted in extra work to make the digital project accessible to your staff and patrons.

There are all types of simple databases you can use to create multiple subject access points to find the images, thereby making the vertical file three-dimensional. Also, the image files should have had some names or identifying information attached to them. You should have created some naming convention so that the files were identifiable without the subject headings. By creating metadata for each image file, you provide a way to access the data without a database or index. You also prevent the image files from being lost when your computer technology staff converts from one system to another over time.

All this is part of protecting your data for current and future generations of users. If you cannot find the data now, how are you going to find it later? What if you want to link the images into your online catalog, so researchers can find out about your rich local history resources? When you approach a digitization project, you need to think about all the potential uses and users for the collection. Careful planning and forethought when creating images will preserve the data and its access methods well into the future.

8

Decision-Making for Today and Tomorrow

Thinking for the Long Term

When the planning phase of your digital project is over, it's time to turn to the serious retention decisions that will ensure the long-term survival of the data and its storage medium. How often will you refresh the data using your preferred method while transferring it to a new storage medium? First you need to decide what method to use to "retain" or refresh the original data and to change the data to accommodate new software applications and new hardware. There are a number of techniques available today, each with its own problems and associated costs.

Copying

The simplest technique but the one with the most future obstacles is copying. Using this technique, which is also called "refreshing," the data is transferred to a new storage medium. For example, files from the original tape are copied to a new tape, or from 5¼-inch or 3½-inch diskettes to CD-ROM. These copies are made without changing the data's format. So if the file was originally created using Word 2.2, then the copy would not have any changes made to it. But this method also means that it may be hard to find a working copy of that operating system and word-processing program. When you try to open the file, if the new program can read the file, then it will tell you the format is older and ask if you want to change the file structure to the new version. As long as you rename the file when you close it, or just close the file without renaming it, you won't lose the older version. Don't forget to make a notation in the "properties" box that the file was originally created in Word 2.2. The caveat with this copying method is that if you allow the computer application to change the file into the new version, then you may lose any special features—including font, tables, images, and layout—that were present in the original. Copying is the technique that is being employed at some of the large data storage repositories, including Iron Mountain, for legal and financial industry records. It will be the data owner's responsibility to retain the old operating systems, software applications, and hardware to access the old data. (See case study 4 at the end of this chapter.)

Reformatting or Conversion

Another common method of transferring data to new storage media is reformatting. Individuals do this all the time when they revise projects, papers, and files. This process entails copying data from one type of application to another, or from one application version to another. For example, you convert a data file from WordPerfect to Microsoft Word XP or from Windows 98 to Windows XP. You might be transferring your files from one type of storage medium to another, such as from a diskette to a CD-ROM. The reformatting process may change the look and feel of the document or database. It may alter tables, margins, and images. Once you save the file in the new version, the old software application cannot read the new file.

Migration

To migrate your files or data, you change from one system platform to another, such as from a proprietary system to an open (nonproprietary) system, or from Microsoft Windows to Linux. Migration means more than just moving the data from one system to another. It also means that you changed the data structure. In simpler terms, it means that you had to redesign the database so that the data could be retrieved using a new set of tools. Those institutions that are switching from one online catalog system to another are "migrating" their data. The integrity of the records may be affected during migration.

Emulation

Emulation employs the use of programs that make the computer "mimic the behavior of obsolete hardware and operating systems."[1] There are some questions about the legality of this method, especially in light of the Digital Millennium Copyright Act. For another discussion of these copying issues, see Gregory S. Hunter's book *Preserving Digital Information.*[2]

Copyright

If your digital resources collection includes only items in the public domain, then copyright will not be an issue for you. However, if you plan to digitize and store unpublished materials or items that are out of print but under copyright, then you and your institution need to explore the restrictions and limitations of the current copyright act with regard to intellectual property rights.[3] (See also checklist 29 for basic questions to consider in regard to copyright.)

In a nutshell, the Sonny Bono Copyright Term Extension Act of 1998 pertains to all works currently under copyright. Under the terms of the act, "all copyright is generally extended for an additional 20 years. The new law applies to all original creative works that are created after January 1, 1978. The length of copyright has been automatically extended to the 70 years after the death of the author or the longest surviving author of a work. Also, if the item was a work for hire, then the term will be 95 years from the year of first publication or 120 years from the year of creation, whichever comes first. If the work was published before 1978 and is still under copyright, then the copyright protection is extended to a total of 95 years from the original copyright date. If the work was unpublished or not registered prior to 1 January 1978, then copyright applies for the life of the author plus 70 years, not to expire prior to 2002."[4]

Libraries and archives are able to take advantage of a special exception in section 108 of the Copyright Revision Act of 1976 that allows an archive or library to create up to three copies of a published or unpublished work that falls under copyright for the sole purpose of preservation and security and deposit for research within an institution. If there is a digital copy of the unpublished work, the archive may not make it available outside the institution. Of course, the library may not benefit financially from such copies. "Subsection (c) authorizes the reproduction of a published work duplicated in facsimile form solely for the purpose of replacement of a copy or phonorecord that is damaged, deteriorating, lost or stolen, if the library or archives has, after a reasonable effort, determined that an unused replacement cannot be obtained at a fair price."[5] This means that your institution can make a digital copy, a preservation photocopy and a microfilm copy, or up to three copies in one format. Today many institutions are making a digital and microfilm copy of their fragile or brittle books. The type of copies you create depends upon the needs of your users.

Section 117 of the Copyright Revision Act of 1976 "permits the owner of a copy of a computer program to make an additional copy of the program for purely archival purposes if all archival copies are destroyed in the event that continued possession of the computer program should cease to be rightful, or where the making of such a copy is an essential step in the utilization of the computer program in conjunction with a machine and that it is used in no other manner."[6]

The Digital Millennium Copyright Act of 1998 (DMCA) doesn't permit you to create a way to get around encryption or a password, or to create software that mimics what the original, obsolete software did.[7]

So how does all this affect long-term storage of digital materials? Copyright and intellectual property rights impose limitations upon the copying, compilation, and long-term retention of born-digital and digitized materials. The issues revolve around changing the format of the digital materials, which includes copying the digital information from one storage medium to another. The laws impact an institution's ability to access the data when the software is no longer available or usable. This second issue is wrapped up in the Digital Millennium Copyright Act and its prohibition of creating "work-around" methods of access. It is not clear yet if emulation software fits under the umbrella of the DMCA.

Jones and Beagrie have written about British copyright and intellectual property rights and how they pertain to copying or refreshing and the issue of copyright. They also discuss the issue of compilation of digital items into a collection and how this impacts upon the rights of the creators and owners of the information.[8]

Copyright and intellectual property rights must be clarified and delineated before embarking upon a digitization project. Consult your institution's legal counsel for advice and assistance in drafting the appropriate memos of agreement.

Retention Decisions

Review the purpose of the digital collection and whether it is a current events collection of files and websites or a historical collection with substantive textual materials. Retention decisions should be based upon the same criteria that are used when deciding what to purchase for a collection or what to deaccession: authority, currency, access points, perspective, and content. Then look at the physical needs of the storage medium and the access needs of the data and how they are related and accessed. You need to decide

what you will keep and what will die a natural death due to lack of attention and maintenance.

Long-Term Retention of Hardware and Software and the Storage Medium

If there is no hardware that will run the digital storage medium, such as 8- and 10-inch floppies or 12-inch laser videodiscs, how will your organization access the data? Will your organization remember to save the last piece of hardware, the software application and program documentation, and the metadata about the data on the storage medium so that someone in the future can access and read it? If the information is important to your organization, shouldn't you bring the data into the future by repetitive copying, reformatting, conversion, and migration to new software versions and new storage media?

Somewhere in the design and planning process for a digital project, you need to discuss who will be responsible for saving and warehousing old hardware and software applications. Discuss this issue with the institution's computer services staff. Make certain you document who is responsible for long-term storage of the hardware and where the items will be stored. At this time, you should discuss whether anyone will be responsible for making certain the hardware works and that you have stored the associated operating system and software applications with your institution's long-term backup or storage provider.

You need to store the physical medium in an environmentally controlled area or with a data storage company. The environment should be constant and stable with a temperature of 68–72° F and a relative humidity between 35 and 50 percent for CDs and magnetic tapes. It is best to avoid freezing the tapes. Excessive humidity can cause metals to rust and magnetic tapes to get moldy.

Preventive Preservation for Digital Information

After you have put in all the effort of planning, designing, and retaining digital collections, you should build in some preventive preservation procedures. Even though your institution is backing up and storing all data and software applications, you might think about archiving the databases and websites so that there are some snapshots of how the data "was" configured. This can be part of your individual backup routine, as discussed in chapter 1. If you plan to retain these backups as part of your archives, then they should be stored with those collections, not overwritten each time you perform a change.

NOTES

1. Michael Day, "Metadata for Digital Preservation: An Update," *Ariadne* 22, www.ariadne.ac.uk/issue22/metadata/.
2. Gregory S. Hunter, *Preserving Digital Information: A How-to-Do-It Manual*, no. 93 (New York: Neal-Schuman, 2000), 57–58.
3. Stuart D. Lee, *Digital Imaging: A Practical Handbook* (New York: Neal-Schuman, 2001), 18–20, 139–45.
4. Liberally quoted and abstracted from "New Terms for Copyright Protection," www.copyright.gov/fls/sl15.html.
5. U.S. Copyright Office, "Reproduction of Copyrighted Works by Educators and Librarians," Circular 21 (revised June 1998), www.copyright.gov/circs/circ21.pdf.
6. Quote from Copyright Revision Act of 1976, as referenced in U.S. Copyright Office, "Executive Summary: Digital Millennium Copyright Act: Section 104 Report" (includes information on sections 109 and 117 of the copyright act), www.copyright.gov/reports/studies/dmca/dmca_executive.html.
7. June N. Besek, *Copyright Issues Relevant to the Creation of a Digital Archive: A Preliminary Assessment*, pub 112 (Washington, D.C.: Council on Library and Information Resources and Library of Congress, 2003).
8. Maggie Jones and Neil Beagrie, *Preservation Management of Digital Materials: A Handbook* (London: British Library, 2001), 32–34, 50–51.

CASE STUDY FOUR

Long-Term Storage and Legal Compliance

For many years now, banks and other financial institutions have been required by the federal government to have contingency plans to get their computer systems back up within 24–48 hours of a system failure. Some of this legislation harks back to the stock market crash of 1929. In fact, given the computerization of brokerage firms and stock trading companies, and the enormous number of trades that occur each day, stock and bond companies cannot really keep up without computers. Okay, so with the help of computers, the financial industry is taken care of for the short-term: minutes, hours, and days. But what about keeping track of trades for the long-term: months and years?

By law, businesses also have to keep track of their records for various periods of time: five to seven years for some records, forever for others, just like your tax return records. For all businesses, this now includes e-mail in addition to all their business transactions, financial records, and correspondence. In the past, businesses just boxed up last year's records and put them into storage, hoping no one would ever ask for them. Today, businesses create and keep most of their records in electronic format. So how will they be able to retrieve those records in the future, many years from now?

There are data storage solutions out in the marketplace that will help businesses store their records and data for the long term. Data vaulting is one method that allows companies large and small to transmit their data electronically to a digital storage facility. These facilities, of which the Iron Mountain Digital Archives is one, provide options for the long-term storage of digital materials.

Iron Mountain's Digital Archives division currently stores data in standard formats such as ASCII, JPEG, and TIFF.[1] The data is transferred to Iron Mountain via electronic data stream or TCP/IP. There Iron Mountain staff and computers store the data for long-term access and retrieval. Their goal is to have the data available when you ask for it, even years into the future. So they will transfer data from one storage medium to another, keeping up with changes in the medium and the hardware that reads it. However, Iron Mountain Digital Archives is not responsible for its clients' ability to read the data, except to make certain the medium is playable. The client itself is responsible for keeping up with changes in software applications and operating systems. If the old data can't be read by newer versions of software application, it is the client's responsibility to reprogram the software or find an emulator. Iron Mountain Digital Archives currently stores all kinds of digital materials, including e-mail, images, forms, office documents, voice files, web content, scanned documents, and video.

In order to take advantage of these digital storage options, the organization needs to think about how it will identify the data in the future. Data can be sent in a sequential order, as in the case of e-mail or a backup file. Unarranged data is expensive and time-consuming to retrieve if a computer technician or a researcher must go through every file to find the information they need or lost. Before sending the data to the data vault, the organization, its records managers, and information technology staff need to think about how they will identify the data in the future. Files need to be created that describe how the data are arranged and what access methods are in use—in other words, metadata. Data that is backed up together with its database and access points will be easier to retrieve if the structure is maintained and documented also.

Many projects are under way that focus on future retrieval and data association techniques. We already know that older tapes and storage media from the 1960s, 1970s, and even 1980s are either unreadable or very expensive to re-create. Only time will tell how effective the new solutions will be.

NOTE

1. More information about Iron Mountain Digital Archives can be found at www.ironmountain.com/services/svc3.asp?svc1_content=4&svc2_code=11&svc3_key=51.

9

The Future

Organizations Involved with the Study of the Preservation of Electronic Records

Libraries and archives and their associated organizations are looking seriously at the issues of long-term preservation. The concepts and practices that they are examining include access to records today and in the future; ways to store the physical medium as well as the data so that it will be readable; and methods of indexing and describing records so that future generations will know what the records consisted of and how they were interconnected.

As scholars and researchers continue to look at the issues of storage and access, they are recognizing the need for all systems of data storage and retrieval to be able to communicate across platforms, formats, and time. Serious money is being funneled into these studies and involves many information-based and scholarly communities, including the Library of Congress and the National Archives in the United States. This is a truly international effort that reaches across the globe and into every discipline. What began as the ability to share data and communicate across platforms with the development of e-mail and file transfer protocols has evolved into international collaboration in studying the description, access, and long-term retention of all types of electronic materials.[1]

The following is a selected list of organizations that are concerned with long-term retention issues involving digital records and their associated storage media. Intellectual content, cross-platform communication, and standardized description and cataloging are just some of the issues these organizations are examining and researching. Postal, e-mail, and web addresses for the organizations described below are provided in appendix A of this book.

ARMA International, the *Association of Records Managers and Administrators*, is an international organization that fosters the organization of information for easy retrieval at all levels of an organization. It works closely with the Society of American Archivists to develop standards for the description and retrieval of electronic records and the cross-dissemination of information between all types of archives and records centers.

The *Association for Information and Image Management's* (*AIIM's*) mission is to "capture, manage, store, preserve and deliver enterprise content to support business processes." The association and its members work in the information management field, organizing and accessing all types of electronic documents and fostering the exchange of digital information.

The *Association of Moving Image Archivists* (*AMIA*) is looking at moving image archival activities, including preservation, cataloging and documentation, and access through education and publication. Its members work with film, video, and electronic formats that revolve around moving images and are interested in long-term storage issues, both physical and digital.

CAMiLEON stands for *Creative Archiving at Michigan and Leeds: Emulating the Old on the New Emulation.* The organization looks at digital preservation issues for data and programs that run on obsolete software, hardware, and platforms. It is also looking at how emulation fits with long-term retention and preservation strategies for digital data. In addition, CAMiLEON is exploring the use of standard programming languages to enable emulation no matter how old the data or software.

The mission of the *Council on Library and Information Resources* (*CLIR*) is to "expand access to information, however recorded and preserved, as a public good." The organization studies issues dealing with the retention and dissemination of information in libraries and other cultural institutions. Preservation issues including storage, reformatting, archiving, and long-term retention are some of the current studies CLIR has undertaken. CLIR makes its publications, reports, and newsletters available on its website (www.clir.org).

The *Digital Library Federation* (*DLF*) is housed at CLIR and focuses on the use of electronic information technologies to extend collections and services in libraries and archives. The DLF is concerned with the structure of electronic resources that are organized into libraries and then are made accessible via the World Wide Web for use by anyone. It is also interested in issues revolving around the archiving of electronic journals.

The *Digital Preservation Coalition* (*DPC*) was founded in 2001 to address the urgent challenges of securing the preservation of digital resources in the United Kingdom and to work with others internationally to secure our global digital memory and knowledge base. The organization provides information about digital preservation and its implementation and importance to the library and archive field. It also promotes all activities related to the preservation of digital information in the United Kingdom and throughout the international community.

The *Electronic Resources Preservation and Access Network's* (*ERPANET's*) mission is to provide education about "how to handle existing digital preservation problems, and how to plan effectively for the future." This European initiative is a cooperative organization designed to provide education and information to European libraries and archives about digital records and their long-term access and storage. ERPANET's website (www.erpanet.org) contains links to papers, presentations, and information on the topic.

The *European Commission on Preservation and Access* (*ECPA*) supports "keeping collections in European archives and libraries accessible over time." It works to raise awareness about the issues of preservation and long-term storage of collections—paper, nonprint, and digital. It works with CLIR and UNESCO to study digital preservation issues and to disseminate reports and studies on the topic. In addition, ECPA provides education for library and archive professionals who deal with preservation but not necessarily conservation of materials in their collections, and it keeps track of European activities that involve preservation. One of its current projects, called EC Project PRESTO, is exploring how to preserve the multimedia archives of European broadcasting organizations.

International Research on Permanent Authentic Records in Electronic Systems 1 (*InterPARES 1*) was organized from 1999 through 2001 "to develop the theoretical and methodological knowledge required for the long-term preservation of the authenticity of records created in electronic systems." The primary focus of this project was to look at inactive archive records: their organization, identification, indexing, and arrangement for long-term access and preservation. The preservation and organization of government, institutional, and individual digital records were considered and recommendations about how to describe and arrange the records were made. Special attention was paid to provenance and maintaining the authenticity of these digital records. *InterPARES 2: Experiential, Interactive and Dynamic Records* will focus on active records storage, arrangement, and access. This part of the project was begun in January 2002 and will continue until December 2006.

JSTOR: The Scholarly Journal Archive states its mission as creating a "reliable and comprehensive archive of important scholarly journal literature."

It is a cooperative, long-term storage repository of journals in electronic format. The journals are available to those institutions that participate in the digitizing project. JSTOR digitizes and then stores the electronic versions of the journals, thereby providing access to journals that some libraries may not own.

The *National Archives and Records Administration Electronic Records Archives (NARA ERA)* provides guidance and standards for the collection, storage, and access of electronic records created by federal agencies and housed at or by NARA. The program is looking at how to integrate access to the records and organize them so that they will be retrievable in the future no matter how the records were created or where they are located. NARA is working with the National Partnership for Advanced Computational Infrastructure to create standards and look at the issues of persistence and long-term access.

The *National Digital Information Infrastructure and Preservation Program (NDIIPP)*, created by the U.S. government, began in 1998 and is run by the Library of Congress. A new initiative and mission began in 2003 to foster "a national, cooperative effort to collect, archive and preserve digital information." The American Memory Project is part of this initiative. The NDIIPP is a public service project of major importance to the nation as well as the world. The NDIIPP recognizes that an enormous amount of information is being created in digital formats or is being digitized. The program focuses on how this data will be stored and accessed in the future. The initiative is encouraging collaborative efforts between institutions and organizations to reduce costs, storage space, create standards, and much more.

The *National Information Standards Organization (NISO)* coordinates the creation and dissemination of standards for all types of data. New standards include how to mark up digital documents, implement XML and SGML, and exchange data across computer platforms so that various systems can read and access information such as MARC tags and cataloging.

The *National Partnership for Advanced Computational Infrastructure (NPACI)* has as its mission to create a national computational infrastructure that describes the relationship between data and their associated infrastructure. Its scientists and researchers are exploring issues of consistency, organization, and the integration of data structures over a wide variety of digital resources and access points. Another project is to look at the persistence of data, that is, how data will be maintained and accessible for long periods of time—regardless of the hardware and software platform—through migration and copying to new formats and storage media.

OCLC Online Computer Library Center sponsors the Dublin Core Metadata Initiative, which is concerned with the "development of interoperable online metadata standards" and encourages organizations to use a controlled vocabulary to describe their libraries' resources in online catalogs. OCLC's research efforts and standards are integral to the organization and interaction of various Internet resources and repositories. Documents, manuals, and publications for implementation of metadata can be found on its website (www.oclc.org). OCLC's Digital Collection and Preservation Services teaches libraries about digitization and long-term access to their digital collections. This service also provides preservation and digitization services. Its goal is to assist libraries with the organization and execution of digitization projects. The Dublin Core Metadata Initiative and the Digital Collection and Preservation Services research best practices and protocols for the long-term retention of materials in cultural institutions.

The *Open Archival Information System (OAIS)* is a structural approach to archives enabling interoperability between programs, platforms, generations, systems, etc. OAIS is supported by ISO and affects many types of information system designs, including digital archives. The OAIS archive model focuses on the documentation of data whether it is print or digital by identifying content; the context in which it is or was used and created; the provenance, i.e., the history and ownership of the data; and the authenticity of the data. The structure is designed to foster long-term preservation of digital objects within their original context or relationships.

The *Open Archives Initiative* (*OAI*) "develops and promotes interoperability standards that aim to facilitate the efficient dissemination of content." The participants work together to develop standards that organizations, businesses, and repositories can use to create, provide access to, and store digital files so that they work across any platform and across time. The emphasis is on interoperability across platforms and programs.

The National Library of Australia's *Preserving Access to Digital Information* (*PADI*) initiative "aims to provide mechanisms that will help to ensure that information in digital form is managed with appropriate consideration for preservation and future access." PADI contains documents and links to organizations that are involved with the preservation of digital materials and resources. PADI is managed by the National Library of Australia with the support of CLIR and DPC. Its website (www.nla.gov.au/padi/about.html) also includes guidelines for descriptive, structural, administrative, and preservation metadata.

The *Records Continuum Research Group* (*RCRG*) is based at Monash University in Caulfield, Victoria, Australia. RCRG examines "methods of analysis which enable records to be controlled at different points in time throughout their life span. This includes the way records are represented, used, retrieved and disseminated. The group is also looking into how continuum models apply to information management and data archiving."

RLG (*Research Libraries Group*) is a member of an international network of expert partners collaborating on the course of digital preservation. RLG committees have been researching long-term storage issues, metadata, and digital repositories found in larger research libraries. They are certifying digital archive repositories that will store electronic resources for scholarly research. RLG is the publisher and distributor of *RLG DigiNews*, a web-based publication that examines digital initiatives.

The mission of the *Society of American Archivists* (*SAA*) is to provide education about the organization, arrangement, appraisal of, and access to unique documents found in archives of all types and sizes. SAA supports a variety of activities, including the standardization of descriptions of electronic records for current and future access and retrieval.

The United Kingdom's Public Record Office and the Historical Manuscripts Commission joined together in April 2003 to form a new organization, the *National Archives*. Information about it can be found at www.nationalarchives. gov.uk/about/default.htm. The National Archives is engaged in collecting and disseminating information to the public in print and in digital format. It has developed schemas, standards, and protocols for the creation, transmission, and storage of digital information and to enhance government interoperability in conjunction with UK GovTalk. The schemas and standards can be found at www.govtalk. gov.uk/schemasstandards/schemasstandards. asp. The U.K. National Archives sponsored the conference "Practical Experiences in Digital Preservation" in April 2003 that focused on digitization, digital preservation, and long-term storage issues, itself along with protocols for delivery and storage of information at the National Archives.

The U.K. National Archives is currently involved in an interesting effort to restore access to the BBC's Domesday Project. On the 900th anniversary of the Domesday Book, which was created by William the Conqueror and described Britain in 1086, the BBC created an enormous digital archive about contemporary life in Britain in 1986.[2] This archive was digitized and stored on the then-current technology of two 12-inch laser videodiscs. What was leading-edge technology in 1986 is so obsolete today that the hardware needed to access it is almost impossible to find, and the storage medium has been superseded by other formats. Paul Wheatley at the CAMiLEON project, Leeds University, is working with emulation software to read and migrate the data on the laser videodiscs to a new format, DigiBetaCam, a digital tape.

Conclusion

Protecting data is a multifaceted problem that requires the creators and keepers of data to be proactive. We must think about keeping data current and backed up for swift recovery after computer failure. We must also think about how to access that data years from now. If we do not plan for the future with disaster response and preservation programs, we lose the past.

NOTES

1. For a history of the development of e-mail and the Internet, see Katie Hafner and Matthew Lyon, *Where Wizards Stay Up Late: The Origins of the Internet* (New York: Simon and Schuster, 1996).

2. More information about the BBC's Domesday Project can be found at www.atsf.co.uk/dottext/domesday. html and at http://news.bbc.co.uk/2/hi/technology/2534391.stm.

10
Checklists

The 29 checklists that follow were created to help you design your data protection plan and organize your efforts to keep track of information about computer hardware, software applications, and the data itself. Checklists 1–11 will help you organize a disaster response plan for your computers. Checklists 12–24 are designed to help you organize information about backups and about individual, network and building hardware configurations, software applications, and data. The remaining checklists include decision-making criteria for long-term retention of electronic resources.

The checklists are guides for creating your own plans. They do not constitute a plan in and of themselves, but are the building blocks for one. You should modify and amend the checklists to make them fit the needs of your institution.

Contents

1. Step-by-Step Basic Disaster Response Action Plan

(Computers crash, virus or worm infection, telecommunications failure or power outage)

☐ Assess the amount of data loss

☐ Determine the type of data access necessary

☐ Determine the duration of outage (or reach maximum waiting time for declaring a disaster—say 30 minutes to one hour for libraries; less than 30 minutes for data-critical operations)

☐ Switch to remote operating location

☐ Switch to manual operations

☐ Declare a disaster

☐ Contact insurance company as to scope of damage

☐ Arrange for software and data to be delivered to remote data center (mobile, hot or cold site)—gather staff

☐ Install the hardware, virus-checking software, software, and data at remote location

☐ Run virus checker to confirm that system is free of viruses and worms

☐ Confirm that the data is accessible and the most current data is available to users. It is important to determine what is most current if the data is backed up continuously.

☐ Check primary location hardware and software for viruses before loading data. Recheck for viruses after data is loaded.

☐ Test the integrity of the system and the data—is the system working properly and is it accessible from remote location?

☐ Return to "normal"

Local Team (on-location)

☐ Switch to remote operating system

☐ Check, clean and/or replace damaged hardware

☐ Install software onto new/cleaned hardware

☐ Check for viruses

☐ Load the data

☐ Check for viruses

☐ Synchronize with remote data system

☐ Return to normal

Alternative Service Locations

- [ ] Access data and software applications from remote/mirror servers
- [ ] Initiate alternative data-collection routines as needed
- [ ] Back up data to remote location
- [ ] Activate manual data-collection routines as needed

Remote Team (at remote recovery site)

- [ ] Order necessary hardware if needed
- [ ] Install software
- [ ] Check for viruses
- [ ] Load data
- [ ] Check for viruses
- [ ] Provide access to remote locations
- [ ] When local system restored, synchronize data

If remote recovery site is secondary location for server and data, then

- [ ] Contact alternative service sites to access data from remote/mirror site
- [ ] Check for viruses
- [ ] Activate data collection for administrative services (fiscal, personnel, etc.)
- [ ] Provide e-mail from remote site if necessary, with virus checker on all incoming and outgoing e-mail
- [ ] Establish additional backup routines for data and software applications to temporary data storage facility while using remote site to provide data access
- [ ] Batch load data from alternative service locations as needed
- [ ] Coordinate restoration of data services at primary site as hardware and software become available
- [ ] Synchronize data at both locations
- [ ] Return service to primary site

2. Alternative Disaster Responses

Loss of Building or Lack of Access to Building

☐ Move all data operations to remote location

☐ Move non-disaster response team personnel to alternative service locations

☐ Assign disaster response team members their responsibilities for recovery

Loss of Telecommunications or Power to Building or Institution

☐ Move all data operations to remote location

☐ Activate manual operations for data collection (circulation desk)

☐ Assign staff to alternative service locations as needed (on or off campus)

☐ Back up all data and prepare for remote access from alternative service locations

Loss of Access or Power to Department or Building

☐ Move all data operations to remote location as needed

☐ Activate manual operations for data collection (circulation desk)

☐ Assign staff to alterative service locations as needed (on campus if possible)

☐ Back up all data and prepare for remote access from alternative service

Water Damage

☐ Turn off all electricity to building or area with water

☐ Turn off all hardware

☐ Activate alternative data operations

☐ Prepare for data access from alternative service locations

☐ Remove standing water from floors and equipment

☐ Evaluate extent of damage to hardware

☐ Replace hardware if destroyed; clean and recertify if just wet

3. Emergency Remote-Access Routines

E-mail access via modem or Web:

_____

_____

_____

Online catalog and electronic resources:

_____

_____

_____

Remote access to intranet:

_____

_____

_____

Include special software and browser configurations for remote access to systems:

_____

_____

_____

4. Computer Assistance Contact Information for Lost Data and Damaged Hardware

Type of assistance	IT contact name	Phone number
Software		
Hardware		
Lost data		
Remote storage of data/software		
System-wide crash		
Virus or worm infection		

5. Hardware Inventory: Needs and Types

List minimum number per building:

_____ Monitors and CPUs or laptops

_____ Printers

_____ Modems

_____ Phone lines

6. Software Inventory: Needs and Types

List minimum number per building or network:

_____ Operating system/type

_____ Software applications

_____ Antivirus software

_____ Office suites

_____ E-mail and/or contact management

_____ Imaging and scanning

_____ Databases

_____ Proprietary program names and types

Identify location of backup copies of application software and license information:

_____

_____

Computer contact person for the building or network:

_____

_____

7. Vendors

Have two companies or contact people for each service.

Type of service	Name of contact	24-hour phone number
Services—programming and analysis		
Software		
Hardware		
Telecommunications		
Remote storage		
Remote location or mirror site		
Disaster recovery company for data and computers		
Disaster recovery company for physical structure and contents		

8. Consortia

	Contact person	Phone number
Local organization		
Statewide organization		
Regional organization		
Statewide online catalog and databases		

9. A Basic Disaster Response or Contingency Plan

☐ Contact information for all computer staff (local, building, and institution-wide)

☐ Identify gathering place to assess the damage and amount of loss of computer software and hardware

☐ Detail frequency and type of backup for each computer and network system

☐ List personnel responsible for backing up the data and software

☐ Contact names for fixing or replacing damaged hardware

☐ Storage location and contact information for backup tapes or files—24-hour (include map and simple directions)

☐ Hot site, cold site, or remote mobile location firm's contact name and number, along with who is authorized to declare a disaster (include map and simple directions)

☐ Contact names for remounting software and data files onto computers

☐ Priority or order for restoring computer services per building and department

☐ Simple written procedures for remounting and re-installing software and hardware

☐ Diagrams that show which computers are associated with which networks and peripheral equipment

☐ Compile inventory of hardware and software by room or department, including serial numbers for hardware, serial numbers and licenses for all software, location of any printed manuals

☐ Emergency contact information for all department heads

☐ Contact information and/or preapproved purchase orders for emergency acquisition of computers (hardware and software)

☐ Review insurance contact person and amount of deductible for computers and rental of space

☐ Assign disaster response team member to document loss, written inventory and visual descriptions of loss for insurance claim

☐ Public Information Office contact information

☐ Emergency contact numbers for restoration of power

☐ Emergency contact number for restoration of telecommunications

☐ Supply information to activate emergency phone numbers

☐ Contact information for all employees—activate phone tree or public service announcement

☐ Contact information for state and local library/archive consortia

10. Disaster Response Team Responsibilities

Team member	Responsibilities	Contact information
Team leader	Supervises day-to-day operations, coordinates priorities and operations, and is liaison with the other disaster response teams and assists trouble-shooter with support	
Remote operations	Retrieves the backed-up data and loads the software applications and data onto remote servers	
Local operations	Recovers the hardware and storage media stored on-site and orders new hardware, if necessary, to facilitate the reconstruction of networks and reconfiguration of hardware	
Troubleshooter (technical assistance or Help Desk person)	Facilitates remote access and assists reference and information staff with questions about temporary or new computer configurations	

11. Organizational Computer Responsibility and Data Creation

Local

Area of responsibility	Number of computers or operations	Contact person
Individual computers or department		

Network

Area of responsibility	Number of computers or operations	Contact person
Department		
Building		
Library or archive		
Records center or institutional archive		
Webmasters or data creators		
Electronic resources		
Database of local resources and holdings		

(Cont'd)

11. Organizational Computer Responsibility and Data Creation (Cont'd)

Institution

Area of responsibility	Number of computers or operations	Contact person
Computing center		
Computer technology (computing infrastructure)		
Digital archive or records center		
Intranet—includes Personnel (Human Resources)		
Financial or fiscal services		

12. Business Resumption Insurance Planning
for Computer Operations

Financial needs: insurance, contingency funds, petty cash, emergency purchase orders, business resumption funds

Who can authorize emergency expenditures?

_____

Is anyone else required to sign checks and purchase orders?

_____

Insurance—computer rider—replacement costs or similar function for computers and equipment

Review and update annually or when new systems and operations are added

Contact information

_____

Deductibles

_____

Inventory of damaged and destroyed equipment

_____

Contract personnel to run emergency operations

_____

Hot site/mobile site contact information and yearly contractual costs

_____

Monthly costs for rental of equipment, location, remote site

_____

13. Manual Circulation Procedures

1. Attach a copy of manual circulation procedures for checkout of materials

2. Attach procedures for batch-loading of circulation information from stand-alone circulation systems

3. Attach procedures for input of circulation records after restoration of computer system (checkout and check-in)

_____

_____

4. Criteria for amnesty from fines: _____

_____

5. Procedures for return of materials to other institutions: _____

_____

_____

14. Documenting Restoration of Data

1. List of people who know how to reinstall software and hardware in the building?

   _____

   _____

   _____

2. Are the procedures written down anywhere?   Yes ☐   No ☐

3. Attach a copy of the procedures

4. How long does it takes to back up the data every day? _____

5. Every week? _____

6. How long does it take to find a lost or accidentally deleted file and restore it?

   _____

7. Attach procedures for restoration of data in sequential backup

   _____

8. Attach procedures for restoration of data in incremental backup

   _____

9. How long does it take to install everything on a new hard drive? *(Allow at least 4–8 hours to restore complete system)*

   _____

10. How much time to reformat hard drive?

    _____

11. How much time to install the operating system and software?

    _____

12. How much time to reload the data?

    _____

15. Access to Backup Data

1. Where do you store the backups?

   _____

2. How much of the system is on the backup tapes? _____

3. And how often do you back up the entire system? _____

4. Where do you store the tapes: on top of the computer, in a "fireproof" cabinet in the room (both bad ideas!), at home, in a physical data storage vault, in the car, with a vendor, at the bank?

   _____

5. At what point do you send the backups from on-site/local to remote storage?

   _____

6. Who can get access to the backups? _____

7. Can you load the backups in a remote location or access the data from an alternative computing center?

   Yes ☐   No ☐   (If yes, attach the procedures)

16. Remote Storage Facility Questions

1. How quickly can you get access to the backups? _____

2. What are the costs and time frames for delivery? _____

3. Do you have to go there to pick up the tapes? Yes ☐ No ☐

4. Are your data arranged in such a way that the storage company can find your tapes? Yes ☐ No ☐

5. Can they send the information via secured data line? Yes ☐ No ☐

6. Can the data storage vendor provide a hot site or remote mobile site if you need it? Yes ☐ No ☐

7. Do they have the hardware to set you up for a "declared" disaster? Yes ☐ No ☐

8. Do you have the insurance coverage for this? Yes ☐ No ☐

9. Can the data storage center find your "remote" or alternative location? Yes ☐ No ☐

17. Backup Routines for Individuals

1. Back up data files regularly

2. Back up critical data files daily

3. Back up e-mail contacts monthly

4. Back up "favorite" websites monthly

5. Back up calendars monthly

6. Run virus check at least once a week—make certain that "live updates" occur and that antivirus software is current

7. Remove little-used data and projects monthly—copy to removal storage medium list

8. Computer software applications or programs

   _____

   _____

   _____

9. Store software application discs in safe location away from computer

10. Store frequently accessed removable storage media away from computer—transfer older storage media to building's computing center

18. Frequency of Backup

Type	Frequency	Storage medium	Storage location	Last backup date
Data				
Database				
Website				
Software				
Operating system				
Obsolete operating system				
Obsolete software applications				

19. Backup Personnel

Contact information	Name	Phone number	Location	Hours

20. Location of Backup vs. "Archiving" or Long-Term Storage by Data Type

Type of data	Local storage of backup for immediate access	Long-term storage at remote location
Correspondence	If current project	When project completed
Database	For current access	For long-term storage and for security backup
Publications	For immediate access	For long-term retention
Financial data	For immediate access/date critical	For long-term retention/fiscal responsibility and auditing
Digital/electronic resources, including images		Remote access acceptable and for long-term retention
Programs and software	Local storage	Remote access
Institutional records/ vital records		Long-term storage
Personnel records		Long-term storage

21. Backup Storage Locations by Department or Computer

Where do you store the backups of current files or data?	Next to or on top of the computer ☐ In a "fireproof" cabinet in the room ☐ At home ☐ In a physical data storage vault ☐ In the car ☐ With a vendor ☐ At the bank ☐
What type of data is on the backup?	
How do you identify what is on each storage medium?	
How frequently do you back up current files?	
How frequently do you back up older files?	
Frequency of transfer of the backups from on-site/local to remote storage	

22. Configuration of Computers for Each Network, Floor, Building, and Location

Type of Hardware for Each Computer

(Make one list for every computer, department, network, and server)

Type of hardware	Name or version	Serial number	Upgrade cycle	Updated inventory and insurance
CPU				
Hard drive				
Internal drives				
Local peripherals				
Printer				
Scanner				
Modem or Internet access method				

23. Configuration of Computers for Each Network, Floor, Building, and Location

Type of Software and Data on Each Computer

(Make one list for every computer, department, network, and server)

Type of software	Name and version	Serial number or license number	Upgrade frequency	Updated inventory and insurance
Operating system				
Software programs				
Antivirus software				
Data types				
Data				
Databases				
Websites				
Electronic reserves				
Indicate types of removable storage medium: disc, tape, diskette, other				

24. Configuration of Computers for Each Network, Floor, Building, and Location

List of Standard Software Applications Installed for Each Department

Type		Department		Exceptions
Application				
Contact manager				

25. Suggested Criteria for Evaluating Restoration Importance

Function	Interdependence	Contents	Priority level
Circulation	Interconnected with online local catalog, web catalog, and cataloging dept.	Includes acquisitions records, current catalog, patron records	First
Circulation	Local catalog only	Patron records, current catalog (no acquisitions)	First
Online local catalog	Circulation	Current holdings	Second
Web catalog	Interconnected with online local catalog, circulation and cataloging dept.	Holdings, patron records, circulation status	First/Second
Financial records	Intranet—fiscal services only	Payroll, budget, pension records, accounts payable and receivable	Depends upon remote backup— Second/Third
Financial records	Stand-alone input station—then sent to third party for payment	Payroll	Dependent upon third party
Personnel	Intranet	Policy manuals, procedures, and other personnel protocols (all digital)	Third/Fourth
Personnel	Internal only	Personnel records and historical employment records (paper and digital)	Fourth
Electronic resources— created locally	Web and online local catalog—local users only	Electronic databases— maintained by institution	Third
Electronic resources via consortium or pay service	Local online and web catalog—state or subscription service	Maintained by third party—remote access available	Third
Outreach services/ bookmobile	Remote access to main circulation system	Stand-alone system	Batch load when system available
Local databases	Electronic resources	Online local catalog	Third
Stand-alone systems			Depends on the number of computers disabled and contents

26. Decision-Making Criteria for Long-Term Retention of Digital Materials

Mission statement for institution as a whole:

_____

_____

_____

Mission statement for library/archive/museum/records center:

_____

_____

_____

Collecting policies:

_____

_____

_____

Anticipated users' needs:

_____

_____

_____

27. Decision-Making Criteria for Digital Projects 1

Source of digital material (print or born digital)	Format	Ownership and provenance	Access method	Backup or master files location

28. Decision-Making Criteria for Digital Projects 2

Name of digital project	conversion technique	Retention period	Backup frequency	upgrade and migration cycle	cost of migration

29. Copyright

1. Is the item in the public domain? _____

2. What format is the item in? _____

3. Are we converting from print to digital? _____

4. Was the item born digital? _____

5. Does the DMCA apply? _____

6. Can the institution convert the object under "fair use"? _____

7. Does the institution own the intellectual rights to the materials? _____

_____

RESOURCES

U.S. Copyright Office—www.copyright.gov/
U.K. Patent Office—www.patent.gov.uk/copy/
Copyright Act, European Union—www.eurorights.org/eudmca/CopyrightDirective.html
Digital Millennium Copyright Act—www.loc.gov/copyright/legislation/dmca.pdf

APPENDIX A

Contact Points
for Organizations
Involved with the
Study of the
Preservation
of Electronic
Records

ARMA International
13725 W. 109th St., Suite 101
Lenexa, KS 66215
Phone: 913-341-3808 or 800-422-2762
Fax: 913-341-3742
E-mail: hq@arma.org.
Website: www.arma.org

Association for Information and Image
    Management (AIIM)
International Headquarters
1100 Wayne Avenue, Suite 1100
Silver Spring, MD 20910
Phone: 301-587-8202; Toll free: 800-477-2446
Fax: 301-587-2711
Website: www.aiim.org/index1.asp

Association of Moving Image Archivists (AMIA)
1313 North Vine Street
Hollywood, CA 90028
Phone: 323-463-1500
Fax: 323-463-1506
E-mail: amia@amianet.org
Website: www.amianet.org

CAMiLEON (Creative Archiving at Michigan and
    Leeds: Emulating the Old on the New Emulation)
Website: www.si.umich.edu/CAMiLEON/
    index. html
    (no other contact information available)

Council on Library and Information Resources (CLIR)
1755 Massachusetts Avenue, N.W., Suite 500
Washington, DC 20036
Phone: 202-939-4750
Fax: 202-939-4765
E-mail: info@clir.org
Website: www.clir.org

Digital Library Federation (DLF)
1755 Massachusetts Ave., N.W., Suite 500
Washington, DC 20036
Phone: 202-939-4761
Fax: 202-939-4765
E-mail: dlf@clir.org
Website: www.diglib.org

This is not a complete list. Inclusion on this list is not an
endorsement. For up-to-date information on these organizations, check their websites or the publications section
of my website at www.mbkcons.com/publications/pub
front.htm.

Digital Preservation Coalition (DPC)
Neil Beagrie, Secretary; Maggie Jones, Coordinator
JISC London Office
King's College, London
Strand Bridge House
138–142, The Strand
London, WC2R 1HH United Kingdom
Phone: 0207 848 2937
Fax: 0207 848 2939
Website: www.dpconline.org/graphics/about/
    index.html

Electronic Resources Preservation and Access
    Network (ERPANET)
Peter McKinney, ERPANET Coordinator
11 University Gardens
University of Glasgow
Glasgow, G12 8QQ Scotland
Phone: +44 141 330 4568
Website: www.erpanet.org/

European Commission on Preservation and
    Access (ECPA)
Royal Netherlands Academy of Arts and Sciences
Kloveniersburgwal 29
P.O. Box 19121
NL-1000 GC Amsterdam, The Netherlands
Phone: ++31-20-551 08 39
Fax: ++31-20-620 49 41
E-mail: ecpa@bureau.knaw.nl
Website: www.knaw.nl/ecpa/

International Research on Permanent Authentic
    Records in Electronic Systems 1 (InterPARES 1)

InterPARES 2: Experiential, Interactive and Dynamic
    Records
Luciana Duranti, Project Director
Suite 301, 6190 Agronomy Road
Vancouver, BC, Canada V6T 1Z3
E-mail: luciana@interchange.ubc.ca
Website: www.interpares.org

National Archives
Kew, Richmond
Surrey, TW9 4DU United Kingdom
Phone: 020 8876 3444
E-mail: enquiry@nationalarchives.gov.uk
Website: www.nationalarchives.gov.uk

National Archives and Records Administration
    Electronic Records Archives (NARA ERA)
8601 Adelphi Road
College Park, MD 20740-6001
Phone: 866-272-6272 and 301-837-0740
Fax: 301-837-0483
E-mail: ERA.Program@nara.gov
Website: www.archives.gov/electronic_records_
    archives/index.html

National Digital Information Infrastructure and
    Preservation Program (NDIIPP)
Library of Congress
Attn: George Coulbourne, LM 637
101 Independence Avenue
Washington, DC 20540
Website: www.digitalpreservation.gov
    The American Memory Project (http://memory.
    loc.gov) is part of this initiative

National Information Standards Organization
    (NISO)
4733 Bethesda Avenue, Suite 300
Bethesda, MD 20814
Phone: 301-654-2512
Fax: 301-654-1721
Website: www.niso.org

National Partnership for Advanced Computational
    Infrastructure (NPACI)
University of California–San Diego
MC 0505
9500 Gilman Drive
La Jolla, CA 92093-0505
Phone: 858-534-5000
Fax: 858-534-5152
E-mail: info@npaci.edu
Website: www.npaci.edu/dice/

OCLC Online Computer Library Center
6565 Frantz Road
Dublin, OH 43017-3395
Phone: 614-764-6000 and 800-848-5878
Fax: 614-764-6096
Website: www.oclc.org
    The Dublin Core Metadata Initiative
    (http://dublincore.org/) is part of OCLC's
    Digital and Preservation Resources
    (www.oclc.org/digitalpreservation/)

Open Archival Information System, or OAIS
(http://ssdoo.gsfc.nasa.gov/nost/isoas),
is based at:
RLG
1200 Villa Street
Mountain View, CA 94041-1100
Phone: 650-691-2333
Fax: 650-964-0943
Website: www.rlg.org/longterm/oais.html

Open Archives Initiative (OAI)
Daniel Greenstein, 202-939-4762
dgreenstein@clir.org
Clifford Lynch, 202-296-5098,
Cliff@cni.org
Website: www.openarchives.org

Preserving Access to Digital Information (PADI)
PADI Coordinator
Preservation Services
National Library of Australia
Canberra, ACT 2600 Australia
Phone: +61 2 6262 1642
Fax: +61 2 6262 1703
E-mail: padi@nla.gov.au
Website: www.nla.gov.au/padi/about.html

Records Continuum Research Group (RCRG)
Monash University
Level 7, 26 Sir John Monash Drive
Caulfield, Victoria 3145 Australia
Phone: + 61 3 9903 1060
Fax: +61 3 9903 2005
E-mail: rcrg@sims.monash.edu.au
Website: http://rcrg.dstc.edu.au/about/index.html

RLG (Research Libraries Group)
1200 Villa Street
Mountain View, CA 94041-1100
Phone: 800-537-7546 and 650-691-2333
Fax: 650-964-0943
E-mail: ric@notes.rlg.org
Website: www.rlg.org
    RLG is the publisher and distributor of
    RLG DigiNews (www.rlg.org/preserv/
    diginews)

Society of American Archivists (SAA)
527 S. Wells St., 5th Floor
Chicago, IL 60607
Phone: 312-922-0140
Fax: 312-347-1452
Website: www.archivists.org

UK GovTalk
Office of the e-Envoy
Stockley House,
130 Wilton Road
London, SW1V 1LQ United Kingdom
Phone: +44 (0) 207 276 3320
E-mail: govtalk@e-envoy.gsi.gov.uk
Website: www.govtalk.gov.uk

Other Organizations Concerned with the Long-Term Preservation of Electronic Resources

Internet Archive
Brewster Kahle, Digital Librarian
    Chairman of the Board
P. O. Box 29244
Presidio of San Francisco
San Francisco, CA 94129-0244
Phone: 415-561-6767
Fax: 415-840-0391
E-mail: info@archive.org
Website: www.archive.org/
    (A 501(c)(3) nonprofit organization focused on
    preserving digital works)

JSTOR: The Scholarly Journal Archive
JSTOR User Services
301 East Liberty, Suite 310
Ann Arbor, MI 48104-2262
Phone: 734-998-9101; Toll free: 888-388-3574
Fax: 734-998-9113
E-mail: jstor-info@umich.edu
Website: www.jstor.org

Ohio Memory Project
Ohio Historical Society
1982 Velma Ave.
Columbus, OH 43211-2497
Phone: 614-297-2589
Fax: 614-297-2546
E-mail: ohiomemory@ohiohistory.org
Website: www.ohiomemory.org/om/links2.html
    (list of links for digitization practices and
    standards)

Society of Imaging Science and Technology
     (IS&T)
7003 Kilworth Lane
Springfield, VA 22151
Phone: 703-642-9090
Fax: 703-642-9094
Website: www.imaging.org

U.K. National Archives, Digital Preservation
     Initiatives
Website: www.pro.gov.uk/about/preservation/
     digital/default.htm
The conference proceedings can be found at:
     www.pro.gov.uk/about/preservation/digital/
     conference/default.htm

Universal Preservation Format Project
     (WGBH–Boston, MA)
Thom Shepard
Website: http://info.wgbh.org/upf/

APPENDIX B

Companies That Protect or Help Cope with the Loss of Digital Materials

Agility Recovery Solutions, U.S. Headquarters
(formerly GE Capital IT Solutions Disaster
Recovery Services)
5324 Highway 85, Suite 700
Forest Park, GA 30297
Phone: 800-567-5001

Agility Recovery Solutions, Canadian
Headquarters
2281 North Sheridan Way
Mississauga, ON L5K 2S3 Canada
Phone: 800-567-5001; Toll free: 905-403-3420
Fax: 905-403-3499
Website: www.agilityrecovery.com
(especially mobile recovery sites)

Belfor USA
Kirk Lively, Director of Technical Services
2425 Blue Smoke Court South
Fort Worth, TX 76105
Phone: 800-856-3333
Fax: 817-536-1167
Website: www.belforusa.com
(electronic data and equipment recovery—
both physical and information recovery
as well as recovery, cleaning, and drying of
paper documents, and mold remediation)

BMS-CAT
303 Arthur Street
Fort Worth, TX 76107
Phone: 800-433-2940
Fax: 817-332-6728
E-mail: info@bmscat.com
Website: www.bmscat.com

Comdisco
6111 North River Road
Rosemont, IL 60018
Phone: 847-698-3000; 800-321-1111
Website: www.comdisco.com

This is not a complete list. Inclusion on this list is not an endorsement. For up-to-date information on these organizations, check their websites or the publications section of my website at www.mbkcons.com/publications/pub front.htm.

Contingency Planning and Management
84 Park Avenue
Flemington, NJ 08822
Phone: 908-788-0343
Fax: 908-788-3782
Website: www.contingencyplanning.com/

DataVault (Global Data Vault Corp.)
170 East 12th St., Suite 10
Durango, CO 81301
Phone: 970-375-0011
Fax: 970-375-0111
Website: www.globaldatavault.com

Disaster Recovery Journal
PO Box 510110
St. Louis, MO 63151
    (Street address: 11131 E. South Towne Sq.
    St. Louis, MO 63123)
Phone: 314-894-0276
Fax: 314-894-7474
E-mail: drj@drj.com
Website: www.drj.com

DRI International
201 Park Washington Court
Falls Church, VA 22046-4513
Phone: 703-538-1792
Fax: 703-241-5603
E-mail: driinfo@drii.org
Website: www.driinfo.org

EMC Corporation
176 South Street
Hopkinton, MA 01748
Phone: 508-435-1000
Website: www.emc.com
    (software and networking systems—data
    mirroring and vaulting)

EVault
1600 South Main Street, Suite 295
Walnut Creek, CA 94596
Phone: 925-944-2422; Toll free: 877-382-8581
Fax: 925-944-9909
Website: www.evault.com/

IBM Business Continuity and Recovery Services
300 Long Meadow Road
Sterling Forest, NY 10979
Phone: 800-599-9950
E-mail: ibmbcrs@us.ibm.com
Website: www-1.ibm.com/services.continuity/
    recover/.nsf/documents/home

Iron Mountain
745 Atlantic Avenue
Boston, MA 02111
Phone: 800-935-6966
Website: www.ironmountain.com
    (off-site data protection and digital archive
    services—long-term storage of both physical
    and intellectual data)

Kroll Ontrack
9023 Columbine Road
Eden Prairie, MN 55347
Phone (toll free): 800-872-2599 and 952-937-5161
Fax: 952-937-5750
Website: www.ontrack.com
    (Ontrack Data Recovery Services is a business
    unit of Kroll Ontrack that provides data recov-
    ery services: magnetic media, computer tapes,
    hard drives, and diskettes)

Message One
420 Research Blvd., Suite 330
Austin, TX 78759
Phone: 512-652-4500
Fax: 512-652-4504
General Information: info@messageone.com
Technical Support: support@messageone.com
Website: www.messageone.com/index.asp

Remote Backup Systems
Suite 1
319 Poplar View Lane West
Collierville, TN 38017
Phone: 901-751-8800; Toll free: 800-945-4491
Fax: 901-854-7411
Website: http://remote-backup.com/

RTI Group
4700 Chase
Lincolnwood, IL 60712-1689
Phone: 800-323-7520 or 847-677-3000
Fax: 800-784-6733 or 847-677-1311
Website: www.rtico.com/tekmda1.html and
www.rti-us.com
(cleaning, inspection, and repair supplies for film, magnetic tapes, and discs; audiovisual storage media and audiovisual equipment cleaners are distributed through RTI Tek Media)

Strohl Systems Group
631 Park Avenue
King of Prussia, PA 19406
Phone: 800-634-2016
Fax: 610-768-4135
Website: www.strohlsystems.com/
(planning and consulting)

SunGard Worldwide
680 East Swedesford Road
Wayne, PA 19087
Phone: 610-341-8790
Fax: 610-341-0108
Website: www.sungard.com/

Bibliography

ARMA International and Society of American Archivists. *Sample Forms for Archival and Records Management Programs.* Lenexa, Kan.: ARMA International, 2002.

Arms, Caroline R. "Keeping Memory Alive: Practices for Preserving Digital Content at the National Digital Library Program of the Library of Congress." *RLG DigiNews* 4, no. 3 (June 15, 2000).

Arms, William Y., Roger Adkins, Cassy Ammen, and Allene Hayes. "Collecting and Preserving the Web: The Minerva Prototype." *RLG DigiNews* 5, no. 2 (April 15, 2001). http://www.rlg.org/preserv/diginews/diginews5-2.html#feature1.

Baca, Murtha, ed. *Introduction to Metadata: Pathways to Digital Information.* California: Getty Information Institute, 1998.

Barbash, Tom. *On Top of the World: Cantor Fitzgerald, Howard Lutnick and 9/11: A Story of Loss and Renewal.* New York: HarperCollins, 2003.

Barry, Rick. "Record Challenges." *Federal Computer Week* (June 9, 2003). http://www.fcw.com/fcw/articles/2003/0609/pol-barry-06-09-03.asp.

———. "Saving the Future Now." *Federal Computer Week* (June 2, 2003). http://www.fcw.com/fcw/articles/2003/0602/pol-barry-06-02-03.asp

Battiata, Mary. "Buried Treasure: Why Has Bill Gates Stashed Millions of the Greatest Images of the Twentieth Century under a Mountain in Pennsylvania?" *Washington Post*, May 18, 2003, W14.

Beagrie, Neil. *National Digital Preservation Initiatives: An Overview of Developments in Australia, France, the Netherlands, and the United Kingdom and of Related International Activity*, pub 116. Washington, D.C.: Council on Library Information and Resources, 2003. http://www.clir.org/pubs/abstract/pub116abst.html.

Beagrie, N., and D. Greenstein. *A Strategic Policy Framework for Creating and Preserving Digital Collections, Version 5.0.* London: Arts and Humanities Data Service, 1998–2001. http://www.ohiomemory.org/om/links2.html.

Bergeron, Bryan. *Dark Ages II: When the Digital Data Die.* Upper Saddle River, N.J.: Prentice-Hall, 2002.

———. "Why Your Digital Data Could One Day Disappear." *Harvard Business School Working Knowledge* (February 11, 2002). http://hbsworkingknowledge.hbs.edu/pubitem.jhtml?id=2767&sid=0&pid=0&t=operations

Besek, June M. *Copyright Issues Relevant to the Creation of a Digital Archive: A Preliminary Assessment,* pub 112. Washington, D.C.: Council on Library and Information Resources, 2003. http://www.clir.org/pubs/abstract/pub112abst.html.

Besser, Howard. "Digital Longevity." In *Handbook for Digital Projects: A Management Tool for Preservation and Access,* edited by Maxine Sitts, 155–66. Andover, Mass.: Northeast Document Conservation Center, 2000. http://www.nedcc.org/digital/ix.htm.

Blythe, Bruce T. *Blindsided: A Manager's Guide to Catastrophic Incidents in the Workplace.* New York: Portfolio, 2002.

Board of Governors of the Federal Reserve System, Office of the Comptroller of the Currency, and Securities and Exchange Commission. "Draft Interagency White Paper on Sound Practices to Strengthen the Resilience of the U.S. Financial System." Washington, D.C. August 30, 2002. http://www.banking.state.ny.us/pr020830.htm#White.

Brand, Stewart. "Ending the Digital Dark Age." In *The Clock of the Long Now: Time and Responsibility—The Ideas behind the World's Slowest Computer,* 81–92. New York: Basic, 1999.

Building a National Strategy for Preservation: Issues in Digital Media Archiving, pub 106. Washington, D.C.: Council on Library and Information Resources, 2002. http://www.clir.org/pubs/abstract/pub106abst.html.

Building and Sustaining Digital Collections: Models for Libraries and Museums, pub 100. Washington, D.C.: Council on Library and Information Resources, 2001. http://www.clir.org/pubs/abstract/pub100abst.html.

Business First "Survey: Firms Unprepared for Operations, IT Outages." *Business First,* March 7, 2003, A27.

Canadian Heritage Information Network. *Collecting and Managing Digital Content.* Hull, Que.: Minister of Public Works and Government Services, 2000. http://www.chin.gc.ca/English/Digital_Content/index.html.

Chapman, Stephen. "What Is Digital Preservation?" Presentation at the OCLC/Preservation Resources Symposium: Digital Past, Digital Future: An Introduction to Digital Preservation, Dublin, Ohio, June 15, 2001. http://www.oclc.org/events/presentations/symposium/.

Chen, Su-Shing. "The Paradox of Digital Preservation." *Computer* (March 2001): 2–6.

Childs, Donna R., and Stefan Dietrich. *Contingency Planning and Recovery: A Small Business Guide.* New York: John Wiley and Sons, 2002.

Cloonan, Michèle V., and Shelby Sanett. "Preservation Strategies for Electronic Records, Round 1 (2000–2001). Where We Are Now: Obliquity and Squint?" A report to the National Historical Publications and Records Commission, University of California, Los Angeles, June 1, 2001. http://www.interpares.org/documents/survey_of_preservation_practices&plans.pdf. Also published in *American Archivist* 65 (spring/summer 2002): 70–106.

Conservation On-Line (COOL) Preservation of Audio Materials. "Resources Related to Preserving Both Digital and Analog Audio." http://sul-server-2.stanford.edu/bytopic/audio/.

Conway, Paul. *Preservation in the Digital World,* pub 62. Washington, D.C.: Council on Library and Information Resources, Commission on Preservation and Access, 1996. http://www.clir.org/pubs/abstract/pub62.html.

Cook, Dennis. "Integrating Internet Recovery." *Contingency Planning and Management* (April 1999): 14–20.

Cravey, Pamela J. "Security of Electronic Files and Systems." Chap. 4 in *Protecting Library Staff, Users, Collections, and Facilities: A How-to-Do-It Manual.* New York: Neal-Schuman, 2001.

Darlington, Jeffrey, Andy Finney, and Adrian Pearce. "Domesday Redux: The Rescue of the BBC Domesday Project Videodiscs." *Ariadne* 36 (July 2003). http://www.ariadne.ac.uk/issue36/tna/.

DeCandido, GraceAnne A. "Digital Disaster Planning: When Bad Things Happen to Good Systems." PLA Tech Note: Digital Disaster Planning. Public Library Association, 1999.

Deegan, Marilyn. *Digital Futures: Strategies for the Information Age.* New York: Neal-Schuman, 2002.

"Disasterproof Your Firm Now—While There's Still Time." *Your Company* (August/September 1997): 10–11.

Duranti, Luciana. "The Impact of Technological Change on Archival Theory." Presentation at the International Congress of Archives, Seville, September 2000. http://www.interpares.org/documents/ld_sevilla_2000.pdf.

Duranti, Luciana, Terry Eastwood, and Heather MacNeil. "The Preservation of the Integrity of Electronic Records." School of Library, Archival and Information Studies, University of British Columbia, Vancouver. http://www.interpares.org/UBCProject/index.htm.

El-Hai, Jack. "Where No Business Is Good Business." *Atlantic Monthly* (August 2000): 22–24.

EMC Corporation. *A Symmetrix White Paper: Disaster Recovery as Business Continuity.* Hopkinton, Mass.: EMC Corporation, 2002. http://www.emc.com/pdf/continuity/c894_disaster_recovery.pdf.

"The Evolution of Contingency Planning: From Disaster Recovery to Operational Resilience." *SunGard World* 2, no. 3 (fall 2003):16–20. http://www.sungard.com/nr/SUNGARD/pdfs/v2-3_1620.pdf.

Finney, Andy. "Domesday Project 1986." http://www.atsf.co.uk/dottext/domesday.html.

Fortier, John. Interview by Bob Edwards. National Public Radio, July 2, 2003. http://discover.npr.org/features/feature.jhtml?wfId=1317777.

Ganong, Ray. "The Emergence of E-Vaulting." *Information Management Journal* (January/February 2003): 20–30.

Greenberg, Jeffrey W. "September 11, 2001: A CEO's Story." *Harvard Business Review* (October 2002).

Greenstein, Daniel, and Suzanne E. Thorin. *The Digital Library: A Biography,* pub 109. 2d ed. Washington, D.C.: Council on Library Information and Resources, 2002. http://www.clir.org/pubs/abstract/pub109abst.html.

Hafner, Katie, and Matthew Lyon. *Where Wizards Stay Up Late: The Origins of the Internet.* New York: Simon and Schuster, 1996.

Hamilton, Tyler. "Digital Amnesia: E-Records Are Getting Lost and a Big Effort Is Under Way to Save Them for Posterity." *Toronto Star,* September 12, 2002.

Harvey, Ross. "Multimedia Preservation—Capturing the Rainbow." Presentation at the Second National Preservation Office Conference, Brisbane, Australia, November 28–30, 1995. http://www.nla.gov.au/niac/meetings/npo95rh.html#roth.

Hawkins, Brian L., and Patricia Battin. *The Mirage of Continuity: Reconfiguring Academic Information Resources for the Twenty-First Century.* Washington, D.C.: Council on Library and Information Resources, Association of American Universities, 1998.

Hedstrom, Margaret. "Digital Preservation: A Time Bomb for Digital Libraries." *Computers in the Humanities* 31 (1998): 189–202.

_____. "Research Issues in Migration and Long-Term Preservation." *Archives and Museum Informatics* 11 (1997): 287–92.

Heslop, Helen, Simon Davis, and Andrew Wilson. *National Archives Green Paper: An Approach to the Preservation of Digital Records.* Canberra, Australia: National Archives of Australia, 2002. http://naa.gov.au/recordkeeping/er/digital_preservation/summary.html.

Higginbotham, Barbra Buckner, and Judith W. Wild. *The Preservation Program Blueprint.* Chicago: American Library Association, 2001. See especially chapter 11, "Microforms, Sound Recordings, Video Formats and New Media," and chapter 12, "Library Systems."

Hoffman, Gretchen McCord. *Copyright in Cyberspace: Questions and Answers for Librarians.* New York: Neal-Schuman, 2001.

Hunter, Gregory S. *Preserving Digital Information: A How-to-Do-It Manual.* New York: Neal-Schuman, 2000.

Institute of Museum and Library Services. "Framework of Guidance for Building Good Digital Collections" (2002). http://www.imls.gov/pubs/forumframework.htm.

"Interagency Paper on Sound Practices to Strengthen the Resilience of the U.S. Financial System" (April 28, 2003). Federal Reserve System Department of the Treasury, Office of the Comptroller of the Currency, Securities and Exchange Commission. http://www.sec.gov/news/studies/34-47638.htm.

"InterPARES Bibliography of the Preservation of Digital Records." http://is.gseis.ucla.edu/us-interpares/bibliography/preservation.htm.

Iraci, Joe. *Disaster Recovery of Modern Information Carriers: Compact Discs, Magnetic Tapes, and Magnetic Disks.* Technical Bulletin no. 25. Ottawa, Ont.: Canadian Conservation Institute, Department of Canadian Heritage, 2002.

Iron Mountain Digital Archives. *The CIO Challenge: Change Disruptive Trends into Business Opportunity.* Boston: Iron Mountain, 2002. http://www.ironmountain.com/File_Uploads/Resource_Items/USA/598_0_Disruptive_Trends.pdf.

James, Michael S. "Fading Bits of History: As Computer Records Replace Paper, Some See Weakness in Record of Our Times." *ABCNews.com* (July 12, 2001).

Johnston, Nicholas. "Plan Approved to Save U.S. Digital History." *Washington Post,* February 15, 2003, E01. http://www.washingtonpost.com/ac2/wpdyn?pagename=article&node=&contentId=A10278-2003Feb14&notFound=true.

Jones, Maggie, and Neil Beagrie. *Preservation Management of Digital Materials: A Handbook.* London: British Library, 2001. http://www.dpconline.org/graphics/handbook/.

Kahn, Miriam. *Disaster Response and Prevention for Computers and Data.* Columbus, Ohio: MBK Consulting, 1994.

Kenney, Anne R., and Oya Y. Rieger. *Moving Theory into Practice: Digital Imaging for Libraries and Archives.* Mountain View, Calif.: Research Libraries Group, 2000. See especially chapter 8 of the related tutorial, "Digital Preservation," at http://www.library.cornell.edu/preservation/tutorial/.

Kuyk, Charlie. "Resolving Business Interruption Claims." *Columbus C.E.O.* (March 2002): 39–40.

Lanzinger, Susan S. *Digital Preservation and Metadata: History, Theory, Practice.* Englewood, Colo.: Libraries Unlimited, 2001.

Lavoie, Brian F. "The Incentives to Preserve Digital Materials: Roles, Scenarios, and Economic Decision-Making." Office of Research, Online Computer Library Center (April 2003). http://www.oclc.org/research/projects/digipres/incentivesdp.pdf.

Lawrence, Gregory W., et al. *Risk Management of Digital Information: A File Format Investigation,* pub 93. Washington, D.C.: Council on Library and Information Resources, Commission on Preservation and Access, 2000. http://www.clir.org/pubs/abstract/pub93abst.html.

Lee, Stuart D. *Digital Imaging: A Practical Handbook.* New York: Neal-Schuman, 2001.

Levy, David M. *Scrolling Forward: Making Sense of Documents in the Digital Age.* New York: Arcade, 2001.

"Library [of Congress] Announces Approval of Plan to Preserve America's Digital Heritage." Press release, February 14, 2003. http://www.loc.gov/today/pr/2003/03-022.html.

Lin, Lim Siew, Chennupati K. Ramaiah, and Pitt Kuan Wal. "Problems in the Preservation of Electronic Records." *Library Review* 52, no. 3 (2003): 117–25.

Long Now Foundation. "Digital Dark Age: Digital Data Loss and Preservation Resources." http://www.longnow.com/10klibrary/darkage.htm.

Marcum, Deanna, and Amy Friedlander. "Keepers of the Crumbling Culture: What Digital Preservation Can Learn from Library History." *D-Lib Magazine* 9, no. 5 (May 2003). http://www.dlib.org/dlib/may03/friedlander/05friedlander.html.

Margeson, Bill. "The Human Side of Data Loss." *Disaster Recovery Journal* (spring 2003): 48.

McGeehan, Patrick, and John Schwartz. "Wall St. Shifts to Backups, but Much Commerce Halts." *New York Times,* August 15, 2003, cyber edition, "The Markets."

Mellor, Phil. "CAMiLEON: Emulation and BBC Domesday." *RLG DigiNews* 7, no. 2 (April 15, 2003). http://www.rlg.ac.uk/preserv/diginews/v7_n2_feature3.html.

Merchantz, Bill. "The True Cost of Downtime," pt. 4. *Contingency Planning and Management* (May/June 2003): 12–16.

Midgley, Chris. "Protecting Your Data, Protecting Your Business." *Disaster Recovery Journal* 15, no. 3 (summer 2002): 54–55.

Mohlhenrich, Janice, ed. *Preservation of Electronic Formats and Electronic Formats for Preservation.* Ft. Atkinson, Wis.: Highsmith, 1993.

Moore, Reagan W. "Knowledge-Based Persistent Archives." San Diego Supercomputer Center Technical Report (SDSC TR-2001-7). http://www.sdsc.edu/TR/TR-2001-07.doc.pdf.

National Archives and Records Administration. "Vital Records and Records Disaster Mitigation and Recovery: An Instructional Guide" (1999). Web edition. http://www.archives.gov/records_management/publications/vital_records.html.

National Archives and Records Administration, Archival Research and Evaluation Staff. "A National Archives Strategy for the Development and Implementation of Standards for the Creation, Transfer, Access, and Long-Term Storage of Electronic Records of the Federal Government." Technical Information Paper no. 8 (June 1990). http://www.archives.gov/research_room/media_formats/strategy_for_electronic_records_storage.html.

National Research Council. *The Digital Dilemma: Intellectual Property in the Information Age.* Washington, D.C.: National Academy, 1999. http://www.nap.edu/html/digital_dilemma/index.html in abridged format.

"National Security of Cyberspace." White House draft document. http://www.whitehouse.gov/pcipb/.

Nebraska Secretary of State. "Records Management Division Guidelines." http://www.sos.state.ne.us/RecordsMgmt/recmenu.htm.

NOW with Bill Moyers (about copyright and intellectual property in the digital age). Transcript from January 17, 2003. http://www.pbs.org/now/transcript/ transcript203_full.html.

Ockerbloom, John Mark. "Archiving and Preserving PDF Files." *RLG DigiNews* 5, no. 1 (February 15, 2001). http://www.rlg.org/preserv/diginews/diginews5-1.html#feature2.

Performance Evaluation of BrightStor Enterprise Backup on Hewlett-Packard 9000 Superdome Server. Chicago: DocuLabs, 2002. http://www3.ca.com/Files/WhitePapers/benchmarks_summary_hp.pdf.

Phan, Monty. "Companies Try to Retrieve Data." *Newsday,* September 19, 2001, A39.

Phillips, John T. "The Challenge of Web Site Records Preservation." *Information Management Journal* (January/February 2003): 42–48.

Pitschmann, Louis A. *Building Sustainable Collections of Free Third-Party Web Resources,* pub 98. Washington, D.C.: Digital Library Federation, Council on Library and Information Resources (2001). http://www.clir.org/pubs/abstract/pub98abst.html.

Porck, Henk J., and Rene Teygeler. "Magnetic Tape." Chap. 4 in *Preservation Survey: An Overview of Recent Developments in Research on the Conservation of Selected Analog Library and Archival Materials,* pub 95. Washington, D.C.: Council on Library and Information Resources, Commission on Preservation and Access, 2000. http://www.clir.org/pubs/abstract/pub95abst.html.

Power, Peter G. "Manage a Crisis, Don't Recover from Disaster." *Contingency Management and Planning Online* (January 2003): 22–26.

Preservation and Digitization in ARL Libraries. SPEC Kit 262. Washington, D.C.: Association of Research Libraries, 2001. Executive summary at http://www.arl.org/spec/262sum.html #execsum.

Rashbaum, William K. "Responding to a Blackout, but on Alert for Terrorism." *New York Times,* August 15, 2003, cyber edition, "NY Region."

Real, Frank J. "Tick . . . Tick . . . Tick: Time Is Money When Recovering Lost Data." *Disaster Recovery* 15, no. 4 (fall 2002): 14–16.

Reed-Scott, Jutta. *Preserving Research Collections: A Collaboration between Librarians and Scholars.* Association of Research Libraries, the Modern Language Association, and the American Historical Association on behalf of the Task Force on the Preservation of the Artifact, 1999. http://www.arl.org/preserv/prc.html.

"Reference Model for an Open Archival Information System: A High-Level Intellectual Framework for Thinking about Persistence and Preservation of Digital Objects." http://ssdoo.gsfc.nasa.gov/nost/isoas/overview.html.

Reilly, Bernard F., Jr. *Developing Print Repositories: Models for Shared Preservation and Access,* pub 117. Washington, D.C.: Council on Library and Information Resources, 2003. http://www.clir.org/pubs/abstract/pub117abst.html.

Reuben, Elizabeth. "Migrating Records from Proprietary Software." *Computers in Libraries* (June 2003): 30–33.

Richtel, Matt, and Simon Romero. "When Wireless Phones Failed, Callers Turned to Land Lines." *New York Times,* August 15, 2003, cyber edition, "Communications."

Rimmer, Matthew. "The Dead Poets Society: The Copyright Term and the Public Domain." *First Monday* 8, no. 6 (June 2003). http://firstmonday.org/issues/issue8_6/rimmer/.

RLG. "The Reference Model for an Open Archival Information System (OAIS)." http://www.rlg.org/longterm/oais.html.

Rothenberg, Jeff. *Avoiding Technological Quicksand: Finding a Viable Technical Foundation for Digital Preservation,* pub 77. Washington, D.C.: Digital Libraries, Council on Library and Information Resources, and Commission on Preservation and Access, 1998. http://www.clir.org/pubs/abstract/pub77.html.

Sanett, Shelby. "The Cost to Preserve Authentic Electronic Records in Perpetuity: Comparing Costs across Cost Models and Cost Frameworks." *RLG DigiNews* 7, no. 4 (August 15, 2003). http://www.rlg.org/preserv/diginews/diginews7-4.html.

Savetz, Kevin. "Data Insurance—Cover Your Most Valuable Assets—The Intangible Ones." *New Architect* (May 2002). http://www.newarchitectmag.com/documents/s=2450/new1017879012973/index.html.

Shapiro, Carl, and Hal R. Varian. *Information Rules: A Strategic Guide to the Network Economy.* Boston: Harvard Business School Press, 1998.

Shepard, Thom. "Digital Archiving: Approaches for Statistical Files, Moving Images, and Audio Recordings—Universal Preservation Format Update." *D-Lib Magazine* (November 1997). http://www.dlib.org/dlib/november97/11clips.html#BOSTON.

———. "Universal Preservation Format (UPF): Conceptual Framework." *RLG DigiNews* 2, no. 6 (December 15, 1998). http://www.rlg.org/preserv/diginews/diginews2-6.html#upf.

Shrieves, Shayla. "Computer's Down Again." *Columbus C.E.O.* (June 2002): 47–51.

Sitts, Maxine K., ed. *Handbook for Digital Projects: A Management Tool for Preservation and Access.* Andover, Mass.: Northeast Document Conservation Center, 2000. http://www.nedcc.org/digital/dighome.htm.

Smith, Abby. *The Future of the Past: Preservation in American Research Libraries,* pub 82. Washington, D.C.: Council on Library and Information Resources, Commission on Preservation and Access, 1999. http://www.clir.org/pubs/abstract/pub82abst.html.

———. "Preservation in the Digital Age." *American Libraries* (March 1999): 36–39.

Soete, George J. *Preserving Digital Information.* SPEC Kit 228. Transforming Libraries 5. Washington, D.C.: Association of Research Libraries, 1997.

Summary at http://www.arl.org/transform/pdi/index.html.

Spangler, Todd. "Disaster Recovery: Expecting the Worst." *Byte and Switch* (April 2, 2002). http://www.byteandswitch.com/document.asp?doc_id=13542&page_number=1.

Spooner, John G. "Dell Foments Floppy's Fall." *CNET News.com* (February 6, 2003). http://news.com.com/2100-1040-983596.html.

"Spotlight on NARA: Building NARA's 'Archives of the Future.'" *Prologue* 33, no. 1 (spring 2001). http://www.archives.gov/publications/prologue/spring_2001_archives_of_the_future.htm.

Sproull, Robert F., and Jon Eisenberg, eds. *Building an Electronic Records Archive at the National Archives and Records Administration: Recommendations for Initial Development.* National Research Council Committee on Digital Archiving and the National Archives and Records Administration, 2003. http://www.nap.edu/books/0309089476/html/.

The State of Digital Preservation: An International Perspective. Conference Proceedings, pub 107. Washington, D.C.: *Council on Library Information and Resources,* 2002. http://www.clir.org/pubs/abstract/pub107abst.html.

Sun StorEdge Network. "Data Replicator Software Boosts Data Center Resilience." Sun Systems (n.d.). See especially chapters 1 and 2. http://www.sun.com/storage/whitepapers/sndr.html.

Thibodeau, Kenneth. "Overview of Technological Approaches to Digital Preservation and Challenges in Coming Years." In *The State of Digital Preservation: An International Perspective,* pub 107. Washington, D.C.: Council on Library and Information Resources, 2002. http://www.clir.org/pubs/abstract/pub107abst.html.

———. "There's Nothing like the Real Thing": Preserving Authentic Electronic Records: The Findings of InterPARES I—Preserving Electronic Records, the work of the Preservation Task Force presented at the Society of American Archivists, June 19, 2002. http://interpares_preservation_tf.pdf.

Trujillo, Shirena. "Data Storage Protects Computer Files. *The Durango Herald,* August 29, 2000. http://www.durangoherald.com/archives/tech0108.htm.

Waters, Donald, and John Garrett. *Preserving Digital Information: Report of the Task Force on Archiving of Digital Information,* pub 63. Washington, D.C.: Council on Library and Information Resources, Commission on Preservation and Access, 1996. http://www.rlg.org/ArchTF.

Weber, Hartmut, and Marianne Dorr. *Digitization as a Method of Preservation?,* pub 69. Washington, D.C.: Commission on Preservation and Access, European Commission on Preservation and Access, 1997. http://www.clir.org/pubs/abstract/pub69.htm.

Wiggins, Richard. "Digital Preservation: Paradox and Preservation." *Netconnect* (spring 2001): 12–15.

Wilder, Brent. "Storage Solutions: Options Abound for Virtual Warehouses." *Business First,* February 7, 2003, A27–29.

Wolf, Milton T., Pat Ensor, and Mary Augusta Thomas. *Information Imagineering: Meeting at the Interface.* Chicago: American Library Association, 1998.

Wright, Richard. "Preserving Europe's Memory: PRESTO Shows How to Preserve Multimedia in the Most Cost-Effective Fashion." *Cultivate Interactive* 7 (July 2002). http://www.cultivate-int.org/issue7/presto/.

Zeichick, Alan. "Building a Dam to Last: Archiving Digital Assets." *EContent* (May 2003): 40–46.

Index

Miriam B. Kahn founded MBK Consulting in 1991 and works with libraries, other cultural institutions, and corporations in planning for, recovering from, and preventing disasters that can bring day-to-day operations to a halt. She has been working in the field of preservation since 1989 and writes and teaches on the subject for library consortia and organizations throughout the Midwest. Kahn is the author of *Disaster Response and Planning for Libraries,* 2d ed. (2002), and other books. She was formerly the preservation officer at the State Library of Ohio and coordinator of online services at the University of South Dakota. Kahn holds an M.L.S. degree from Queens College and an M.A. in history from Hunter College.